Sex Cells

Anna Longaretti

A SAMUEL FRENCH ACTING EDITION

SAMUELFRENCH.COM
SAMUELFRENCH-LONDON.CO.UK

FOR PRODUCTION ENQUIRIES

UNITED STATES AND CANADA

Info@SamuelFrench.com
1-866-598-8449

UNITED KINGDOM AND EUROPE

Plays@SamuelFrench-London.co.uk
020-7255-4302/01

Each title is subject to availability from Samuel French, depending upon country of performance. Please be aware that *SEX CELLS* may not be licensed by Samuel French in your territory. Professional and amateur producers should contact the nearest Samuel French office or licensing partner to verify availability. For stock/ professional licensing enquiries please contact Samuel French.

MUSIC USE NOTE

Licensees are solely responsible for obtaining formal written permission from copyright owners to use copyrighted music in the performance of this play and are strongly cautioned to do so. If no such permission is obtained by the licensee, then the licensee must use only original music that the licensee owns and controls. Licensees are solely responsible and liable for all music clearances and shall indemnify the copyright owners of the play(s) and their licensing agent, Samuel French, against any costs, expenses, losses and liabilities arising from the use of music by licensees. Please contact the appropriate music licensing authority in your territory for the rights to any incidental music.

IMPORTANT BILLING AND CREDIT REQUIREMENTS

If you have obtained performance rights to this title, please refer to your licensing agreement for important billing and credit requirements.

SEX CELLS was first produced by Anna Denton for Coy Content at the Riverside Studios, Hammersmith, London in October 2013. Executive producers were Joe Denton and Mark Denton. Original music by Saskia Rothstein Longaretti.

The performance was directed by James Barry and designed by Tina Gardiner, with lighting, sound and stage management by Claire Bradley. The casting director was Annie Rowe, scenic artist Magnus Irvin, assistant director Niall Phillips, assistant stage manager Danielle Hurley and production assistant Caroline Milsom. The cast was as follows:

LILY	Jean Perkins
SYLVIE	Alison Pargeter
JANICE	Kate Russell-Smith
TIFFANY	Serena Giacomini
MR CAUSEWAY	Tom Butcher

CHARACTERS

LILY, 65. Her dress is shapeless and nondescript and her hair is pinned to keep the curl in. She wears pop socks and changes into slippers when she gets to work.

SYLVIE, 39. French (with an accent), slim build, smartly dressed and immaculately groomed.

JANICE, 38. She has a Northern accent, is unintentionally dishevelled (as the main objective was to look glamorous) and looks like she is wearing clothes that she bought when she was younger and slimmer. Her massive handbag is always overflowing.

TIFFANY, 29, slim, Essex girl fashion and accent.

MR. CAUSEWAY, 55. A beanpole of a man. He is old-fashioned in his dress and manner. He wears a thick ribbed cardigan with pockets. He is hardly ever without a cup of tea on the go.

PRODUCTION NOTES

The author would like the words of *Sex Cells* to be said as written

All characters use the correct pronunciation of Aphrodite, ie. 'Af-roh-dy-tee.'

The brackets at the end of some sentences indicate what the character could go on to say (usually when the dialogue is fast-paced). Therefore, these can be vocalised or not.

The set can be made to work how best suits, but the author has some items that can be hired for a run. Please contact Samuel French for more information.

The music that was written for the original production is optional. Please contact Samuel French for more information.

An interval is optional.

TIMELINE

Act One

Scene 1 End of July
Scene 2 Beginning of August
Scene 3 Mid August
Scene 4 End of August
Scene 5 Beginning of September
Scene 6 Mid September

Act Two

Scene 1 End of September
Scene 2 Beginning of October
Scene 3 Mid October
Scene 4 Beginning November
Scene 5 Mid December

CHARACTER NOTES

LILY
Keeps her emotions in check and tries not to feel too much. She is uncomfortable with intimacy and any physicality; she has lived without it for a very long time. Her humour is a coping mechanism. She is brusque and even caustic but her heart is in the right place. She dislikes the fact that Sylvie displays her emotions with abandon. Her feelings towards Tiffany are motherly and protective but she would never give advice – she doesn't feel that she is in a position to give anyone advice. When forced to face reality, her intelligence helps her cope.

SYLVIE
Is a dreamer and perfectionist who wants to maintain control. She needs to present a front to the world that she herself can believe in. Her isolation comes not only from the fact that she is from another country, but that she can't do what she is biologically 'meant to'. She is surrounded by people trying to enhance their sex lives just for the fun of it and often feels like she is the only person in the world who remembers that the sex act is meant for procreation. Having spent so long thinking about her own need she is totally unprepared when the baby arrives and she sees that the baby's need is greater than hers.

JANICE
Can't catch up with anything in her life – there's a desperation about her. She feels guilty for needing time away from her kids and for envying Tiffany's carefree existence. In some ways she is relieved to have Sylvie, whose predicament helps remind her that she has a lot to be grateful for. She listens to endless rows at home so she'd do anything to stop one from kicking off at work.

TIFFANY
Is the most present of all of the women. She is not living in a dream world, has weighed up the pros and cons of what having a child means and knows it's not for her. She has a "live and let live" outlook on life. To fulfil her need to be loved by a man is her overriding aim. She does get let down, but is never down for long: life is for living. The relationship she has with Lily is uncomplicated and easy-going.

MR. CAUSEWAY
Is measured in everything and has weathered years of loneliness. He has a shedload of facts at his disposal that he has no trouble remembering. He could have done something more suited to his intelligence, but a lack of self-worth got in the way. Not only is he in total admiration of Lily's forthrightness, but as someone who has been starved of 'being looked after', no one could appreciate Lily's food parcels more. He feels that he alone 'gets' how good she is, and this knowledge sustains him in his unrequited love.

For Saskia

What joy you have brought to my life

With love and gratitude to Mark,

for helping to make my dreams come true

ACT ONE

Scene One

(A dingy call centre, present day.)

(The stage is split into three parts.)

(The central and largest area is the CALL CENTRE. There are four cubicles or cells where operators answer questions from customers wanting to buy sexual aids. Each cell has a chair, a ledge (which serves as a desk), a screen (on the fourth wall maybe) and a keyboard (which doubles up as a telephone keypad) and an operator headset (single). There is a red light above each cell which flashes when a call is waiting to be answered, and is lit for the duration of the call. Each operator has a button on the keyboard which answers or ends a call. A wall chart shows that Lily is 'sales person of the month' continuously from January to June. Upstage is a set of coat hooks plus tea- and coffee-making facilities on a counter top that houses a sink. A logo on the back wall reads 'Aphrodite'.)

(When the women are not answering the phones they are processing the orders that come in online or sorting through 'returns'. They do this at a table which has a box of latex gloves on it and various sexual aids. An Aphrodite catalogue is available in each cell, for reference purposes.)

(There is a door upstage left which leads to an off-stage corridor leading out onto the street.)

(The section stage right is the BATHROOM.)

(The bathroom consists of a wash basin, the back of which is on the fourth wall, and there is an imaginary mirror above it. Upstage of this is the door to the toilet cubicle.)

(Stage left of the call centre is a door which leads into Mr Causeway's OFFICE, which is almost always open. There is a hatch in the wall of his office which opens onto the call centre.)

(The office is full of box files and general office paraphernalia plus a switchboard, desk, two chairs, notices and rosters which are pinned to the notice board.)

(There are boxes of stock in differing sizes, and have differing labels. They can change between scenes to show the passing of time.)

(The play starts in darkness.)

(Just before each character speaks here, the red light above their cell flashes. As they hit the keyboard to answer the call, the red light burns steadily and the monitor lights up to partially illuminate the character's face. This happens one at a time with each character plunging back into darkness after their opening line is delivered.)

LILY. Aphrodite, goddess of sexual rapture, how can I help?

SYLVIE. Aphrodite, goddess of sexual rapture, 'ow can I 'elp you?

TIFFANY. Aphrodite, goddess of sexual rapture, how can I help you?

JANICE. Aphrodite, goddess of sexual rapture, how may I help you?

(The women are seated in the cells and are wearing the headsets.)

*(Lights up on **LILY**.)*

(She is knitting.)

LILY. The Clitoral Stimulator is twenty-five ninety-five… It's your basic G-string but with rotating pearls… Comfortable? Oh very, I'm wearing mine as we speak… Oh I don't think you'll have a problem on that front… How many? …I'd say about ten a day… You just jiggle about a bit.

(Lights up on **SYLVIE**, *who is more preoccupied with her diary than the caller.)*

SYLVIE. Banana, strawberry, chocolate, chocolate mint… What?… The biggest one, king size… *(flat)* Fourteen inches, really?… No thanks, this is the night that I am washing my hair—

*(***SYLVIE** *hangs up.)*

(Irritated) Idiot!

(Lights up on **TIFFANY**.*)*

TIFFANY. Wait a sec. *(She flicks to the right page in the catalogue.)* The Venus Guy Trap has perfume with pheromones, lubrication oil with pheromones, hair spray, fake tan and some vajazzle crystals in the shape of a heart, it's well cool… It's dear but the crystals are them Swarovski *(has trouble saying it)* them really posh ones—

(Lights up on **JANICE**.*)*

JANICE. Jim! What you doing ringing this number?… What?

(She picks up her mobile and sees it was on silent.)

Oh! Sorry, I had it turned off for assembly… They're on top of the tumble dryer. Turn them inside out just in case they're still wet, *damp*! They may be a bit damp, I've got to go love.

(Lights up on **MR. CAUSEWAY**'s *office)*

(We see him sitting at his desk, bent over a mountain of paperwork.)

(All the women speak at once, creating a cacophony of noise.)

TIFFANY. Forty-one pounds… Can I have the long number on the card? Seven, six, five, eight. And the expiry date?… Security code? …so that's three Titivators and a Teasey Maid, they'll be with you by Thursday. Ask for Tiffany if you've got a problem. Sweet.

JANICE. Aphrodité, goddess of sexual rapture, how may I help you? Yes, sir, the anti-bacterial toy cleaner, small or economy? Two hundred and fifty or six hundred mill… Great, do we have your details on our system?… What's the code?… Thanks, goodbye.

SYLVIE. Aphrodité, goddess of sexual rapture, 'ow can I 'elp you?… The Enlarger is a very popular item, but then the Lust Buster Vacuum pump is very powerful, it depends on what you need?… No, I meant that it enhances the normal erection… Oh fine.

LILY. I tell you what, I can put some anal lube in with the Double Mini Dong and that will take it up to sixty-nine pounds which entitles you to free delivery… Can I have the long number on the front of the card? Six, five, one *(numbers under her breath)* and the expiry date?… And finally, the three digits on the back of the card. Lovely speaking to you, dear. I'm Lily if you need any help in the future.

*(**LILY** goes out the back to collect a returns box. **SYLVIE** watches her go – she is brimming with excitement.)*

SYLVIE. I could do with that kind of commission at the moment.

*(**JANICE** nods in agreement.)*

And I never see her wearing any new clothes—

JANICE. I know, those dresses are so out they're almost in.

*(**TIFFANY** goes to the returns table and dons a pair of Latex gloves ready to examine the returned goods.)*

*(**SYLVIE** uses the fact that **LILY** and **TIFFANY** are out of earshot to have a private conversation.)*

SYLVIE. I have a special reason.

(SYLVIE strokes her tummy.)

JANICE. Are you?

(SYLVIE gives an excited nod.)

SYLVIE. I know I'm supposed to wait but I can tell you.

JANICE. Please god this time, eh?

SYLVIE. I saw some beautiful knitwear at the weekend. I didn't buy it, I'm not going to make that mistake again.

JANICE. I bought knitwear for Trudy. What you want is machine washable.

SYLVIE. I don't care about being practical.

(LILY enters and puts a returns box on the table.)

TIFFANY. We were just talking about you.

LILY. I thought my ears were burning.

(TIFFANY looks at LILY.)

TIFFANY. They're not red or nothing, Lil.

LILY. It means you're being talked about, Tiffany, and people don't talk about you unless there's something worth talking about.

TIFFANY. I hate being talked about.

LILY. They're not talking about you, dear.

TIFFANY. I flippin' hope not.

JANICE. We were discussing your sales technique.

LILY. I only sell 'em what they want.

(TIFFANY takes a realistic pink dildo from under the returns table and glances at the complaint letter that accompanies it.)

JANICE. *(mild complaint)* Did the man who rang up for the Fetish Fantasy Door Swing want the Prince Albert as well? I don't think so.

LILY. *(matter-of-fact)* Well, he was obviously heading that way. He's probably getting it pierced as we speak.

(TIFFANY waggles the dildo.)

TIFFANY. Ouch! *(Pause)* 'Ere, Sylvie wants to know why you always wear the same old clothes, Lil?

*(**SYLVIE** swivels round in her chair.)*

SYLVIE. No I don't.

LILY. Does she now?

SYLVIE. I was just passing the conversation.

TIFFANY. I wasn't trying to land you in it—

LILY. Didn't think I was on your radar, I am flattered.

JANICE. *(diffusing)* We're only envious, aren't we, Sylvie?

*(**SYLVIE** peruses a baby catalogue.)*

TIFFANY. I like finding *bargains* for 'em.

LILY. We are providing non-essential items, Tiffany, it's not like running down to your local Tesco and buying toilet paper and milk.

TIFFANY. I don't go Tesco, I'd have to get the bus. Anyway I've got Lidl's at the end of my road.

JANICE. I try to make them feel special but it doesn't make any difference.

LILY. They can smell the desperation, Janice.

JANICE. God, is it obvious?

TIFFANY. Oh, do me, do me, how do I come across?

LILY. You're bright, airy and vapid, which makes you easy to talk to, I suppose. You do alright don't you?

TIFFANY. *(thrilled)* Aw that's nice. Now do Sylvie, then someone should do Lily.

SYLVIE. She doesn't think of them as people.

*(**JANICE** stands up quickly.)*

JANICE. Who wants coffee?

*(**JANICE** proceeds to make four coffees.)*

*(At the sound of food or drink, **MR. CAUSEWAY** never wastes time. He pops his head out of the hatch.)*

MR. CAUSEWAY. Wouldn't say no.

JANICE. I probably shouldn't have any coffee, I'm not getting much sleep, but—

(**MR. CAUSEWAY** *enters the call room.* **LILY** *and* **TIFFANY** *raise their hands to accept.*)

TIFFANY. You havin' one, Sylv?

(**SYLVIE** *ignores her.*)

LILY. *(to* **SYLVIE***)* Hello? She's making it in the contraption. *(To* **JANICE***)* You're making it in the contraption aren't you?

JANICE. Yes.

SYLVIE. What? No, not today.

LILY. It was your idea to get a cafeteria in the first place.

JANICE. Milk and sugar, Lily?

LILY. What's up then? *This* one not good enough now? She probably wants the one George Clooney advertises.

JANICE. Lily?

LILY. You know how I take it, Janice, don't get your knickers in a twist.

SYLVIE. Caffeine reduces muscle activity in the fallopian tubes that carry eggs from the ovaries to the womb and can double the risk of miscarriage.

(**MR. CAUSEWAY** *winces and goes back to his office, pronto.*)

LILY. Well I did ask.

MR. CAUSEWAY. I'll take my coffee in here.

(**SYLVIE** *takes a silent call.*)

TIFFANY. I could take you shoppin' Lil.

LILY. Spare me.

TIFFANY. I'm wicked at shoppin', all me mates say so.

LILY. I don't waste my money.

JANICE. We don't waste a thing in my house, we can't afford to.

LILY. Have you got a place where you keep elastic bands and string?

(**TIFFANY** *laughs.* **JANICE** *looks on in disbelief.*)

TIFFANY. Jokin' in't ya?

LILY. I do. And buttons and zips, tin foil, old sheets. I haven't bought a cleaning cloth in years.

TIFFANY. Do you really keep string? That's hilarious, I can just/[imagine]—

LILY. – Not laughing when you come to me for money for your you-know-what, are you?

(**TIFFANY** *gasps.* **SYLVIE** *turns her back.* **LILY** *turns to* **TIFFANY**.)

How many times is it now?

TIFFANY. Shhh, you know what I'm like, it's an accident.

LILY. An accident. You can't call *three* an accident.

TIFFANY. Shut up.

(**MR. CAUSEWAY** *enters the call room to wash his mug.*)

MR. CAUSEWAY. What accident?

LILY. Nothing, we were just talking about how some people get a prang very easily *(looks at* **TIFFANY***)* and others hardly ever get pranged at all, *(looks at* **SYLVIE***)* weren't we Tiff?

TIFFANY. Err?

JANICE. *(disparaging)* You should take precautions, or are you always drunk?

TIFFANY. I do, but they don't always work and guys don't like, you know… *(looks at* **MR. CAUSEWAY***, embarrassed)* the other.

JANICE. *(sarcastic)* Oh well, if *men* don't like it!

TIFFANY. I just said it wouldn't make no difference.

LILY. Have you ever thought how you'd do less damage if you got pranged up the bumper?

(**TIFFANY** *clasps her hand over her mouth and* **JANICE** *laughs involuntarily.* **SYLVIE** *tries to ignore the whole topic.*)

MR. CAUSEWAY. I know from bitter experience what it's like to be rear-ended.

(**TIFFANY** *laughs out loud.*)

TIFFANY. Do you, Mr. Causeway?

MR. CAUSEWAY. Oh yes, Tiffany, and it wasn't a laughing matter, I can assure you. I was but a learner.

TIFFANY. Right.

MR. CAUSEWAY. It nearly put me off for good, but it taught me to be cautious and fortunately it hasn't happened since.

TIFFANY. Shame.

MR. CAUSEWAY. Yes. What?

TIFFANY. I meant shame it happened an' that.

MR. CAUSEWAY. Well now you know for yourself, having just had the same experience. Anyway, how can you gauge financially whether it's better to be pranged up the rear end or head-on? Surely the odds are equal? Either way you shouldn't drive whilst drunk, Tiffany. Even one drink can be too many if you are susceptible to alcohol.

(**TIFFANY**, **LILY** and **JANICE** *give each other knowing looks.*)

TIFFANY. Yes, Mr. Causeway.

MR. CAUSEWAY. It impairs judgement and slows reactions. You may not think it does, but it's a proven fact that it does.

TIFFANY. No, Mr. Causeway.

MR. CAUSEWAY. I suggest that if you intend going out for a good time, don't take the car. You won't be having a good time in the morgue, will you? Have you ever driven, Lillian?

LILY. Put it this way, I know the theory, but I haven't done it in years. Not since much past me wedding night if you must know.

*(**TIFFANY** and **JANICE** look horrified. **SYLVIE** clocks their reaction.)*

TIFFANY. God! Really?

JANICE. Really?

MR. CAUSEWAY. Oh, it's not unusual. I heard you say so yourself, Tiffany, some men don't like it. They find independence in women a challenge to their masculinity. Your husband didn't like you driving, Lillian?

LILY. No, and he wasn't a very good driver. Not that *I'm* an expert or nothing.

MR. CAUSEWAY. Yes, I personally think that independence in a woman is *very* attractive.

LILY. From what I can remember, I'm not missing much *(looks to **TIFFANY**)* ***not*** driving.

MR. CAUSEWAY. I wouldn't mind if a wife of mine drove.

*(**TIFFANY** takes a blow-up doll out of a returns box, ostensibly to examine it for punctures. She puts it into a provocative position facing **MR. CAUSEWAY**.)*

TIFFANY. You've never been married, have you, Mr. Causeway?

MR. CAUSEWAY. No, I never found the right woman.

*(He turns away from **LILY** and coughs.)*

I'll just…um—

*(**MR. CAUSEWAY** exits the call room and enters his office.)*

TIFFANY. Ah, bless. *(Pause)* 'Ere, what you doing for your birthday next week, Lil?

LILY. Cooking Bill's dinner like every other night.

TIFFANY. Why doesn't Bill take you *out* to dinner?

LILY. Never met him, have you?

*(**TIFFANY** shakes her head.)*

Well he reckons he's got a bad back and *says* he can't walk very well. That's his excuse for never getting off his arse and expecting me to do everything. Plus the fact that he's a fucking lush and an embarrassment to be seen out in public with, I'd rather not.

TIFFANY. Do you still love him?

(LILY *peers at* TIFFANY *over her knitting.*)

I'm just interested. You know, to see if you can still be in love after years and years of/[marriage]—

LILY. If you must know, it's thirty-six years and I can't remember ever lovin' him.

TIFFANY. Why d'you marry him?

LILY. I was up the duff, first time we did it, so we had to get married. It's what we did in them days.

JANICE. Bloody hell.

LILY. *(mournfully)* I wouldn't mind but he only waggled it about a bit. It never even went in properly. Least not as far as I could tell, what with me being unspoilt and all. *(Sad)* Bit like trying to shove a marshmallow into a slot machine. Never dreamt I'd fall pregnant after that poor excuse for a fuck. *(Perking up)* I was obviously very ripe, what can you do? *(To* TIFFANY*)* I was a bit like you in that way.

(TIFFANY *can't help but agree.*)

JANICE. Is this really the kind of subject—?

SYLVIE. It's fine, I'm fine Janice.

LILY. *(surprised)* Makes a change.

SYLVIE. It's impossible to upset me today.

(LILY *notices that* SYLVIE *has a holier-than-thou countenance.*)

LILY. Oh, I get it. Well we can all breathe a sigh.

(SYLVIE *makes a non-committal shrug but is pleased to be noticed.*)

LILY. *(to* TIFFANY*)* You *ever* going to want a nipper?

TIFFANY. Nah.

JANICE. How come?

TIFFANY. My twin right, with her two, looks well haggard and I'm not allowed to call after nine 'cos she's in bed. And since my mate Jak's had a kiddie, *we never see her* and she used to *love* clubbing. And, right, in *Who's Doing What* magazine, it said how Russell Brand and Katy Perry split up yeah. Well they split up because he wanted to have kids and she didn't want to have them and if I was Katy Perry—

JANICE. – My God I thought she was going to say something groundbreaking for a minute.

TIFFANY. No, wait right, 'cos if I had her looks and figure, and her career, I wouldn't want to blow it all either. You have to be really grown up and put them first and everything.

LILY. She's not as stupid as she looks—

TIFFANY. Far as I can tell, they fuck up your life and that.

JANICE. So essentially you're saying that my life's over because I've got kids?

TIFFANY. No, I didn't mean it for you—

JANICE. Oh because my figure is shot to pieces and not worth preserving.

TIFFANY. – No, no, I … I didn't mean it like that, I just meant for me.

JANICE. – 'Cos your figure *is* worth it I suppose?

TIFFANY. – No, look, I'm really sorry.

LILY. Leave her alone, she wasn't having a go at you Janice.

JANICE. But it's alright for you to comment on Sylvie's situation though.

LILY. Pardon me, I don't know if you've noticed, this is not a big room, claustrophobic some might say, and none of us know what we can and cannot mention in front of, you know who parlez-vous. She's so bleedin' tetchy.

SYLVIE. *(sarcastic)* I'm sorry to be such a pain.

JANICE. You'd be tetchy – (too if)

SYLVIE. – Yes well I hope I finish with all of that now.

(Pause)

(And the penny drops for **TIFFANY***.)*

TIFFANY. *Oh!* You're *pregnant*! I wondered why you was being like that.

SYLVIE. *(delighted)* I am not counting the chickens.

TIFFANY. When's it due?

SYLVIE. December the sixteenth, *if* it all goes well. Sagittarius.

LILY. Saggy-hairy-arse.

JANICE. Lily!

SYLVIE. It's alright, Janice. I will have to get used to dealing with people making fun for their children, I suppose that's what mothers do.

JANICE. It's fun *of* their children and *yes*, it's agony.

SYLVIE. No one said it would be easy.

LILY. I've never known anyone want one half as bad as you do. Far as I'm concerned there's enough of us on the planet as there is.

SYLVIE. Why does anyone want a baby? It's perfectly natural.

LILY. I don't class sticking needles in yourself as *natural*.

(Lights on **SYLVIE** *in a Madonna and baby kind of way.)*

SYLVIE. Maybe, but I go through it. The treatments, the hope, the disappointments, so that *one day* I'll be able to hold my baby in my arms, to pour all of my love onto her, to bring a life into the world and give the things I never had. To fulfil the role I'm meant to, to be a mother, to be a woman, to put right the wrong. And for that I would do anything. *(She imperceptibly touches her belly.)*

(Respectful pause)

(Lights up)

LILY. Fuck me! Did you read that off the back of a packet of Cow and Gate?

*(***SYLVIE** *gasps and rushes to the bathroom.)*

What?

JANICE. Honestly!

(JANICE *follows* SYLVIE.)

LILY. We should get her phone installed in there.

(TIFFANY *knows it was cruel but can't help laughing.*)

TIFFANY. Aphrodite, goddess of sexual rapture… Donna? No, sorry mate, there's no Donna works here. What? … Oh, you want the kebab house, it's *seven*, nine, one two… Cheers.

(LILY *enters* MR. CAUSEWAY*'s office with dockets in her hand. He takes the dockets and remembers that he has something for her. He hands her a clean piece of Tupperware. She accepts it but he continues to hold onto it.*)

MR. CAUSEWAY. That was a nice shepherd's pie, thank you Lillian, I finished it off with the lemon drizzle cake and a cup of tea.

LILY. You're welcome.

MR. CAUSEWAY. I went to a Michelin-starred restaurant once and the cooking wasn't as good as yours.

LILY. You've said, it's nice to be appreciated.

(*Uncomfortable with the compliments, she tries to leave, but he's still holding on.*)

MR. CAUSEWAY. It's unfussy but wholesome and full of flavour.

LILY. My Bill complains if it's not on the table on the dot of six-thirty and he only comments when something's not right… It's only leftovers anyway.

(*She tries to leave, but he's unaware.*)

MR. CAUSEWAY. No one has leftovers every single day.

LILY. Someone's got to fatten you up and I can imagine the kind of thing you'd cook left to your own devices. Actually I don't have to imagine, I've seen your *lunch box.*

(MR. CAUSEWAY is used to LILY's jokes, they are usually like water off a duck's back. He realises he has hold of the Tupperware and lets go.)

MR. CAUSEWAY. Oh. Er, I was trying to decide, of all your cakes I'd say the ginger is my favourite.

LILY. Unusual choice.

MR. CAUSEWAY. I know, but then I've never liked the same things as the mainstream.

LILY. I'd guess that most people would choose a Victoria sponge.

MR. CAUSEWAY. I've always been a bit different.

LILY. You can say that again.

(She tries to leave.)

MR. CAUSEWAY. Not everyone can take the heat of the ginger and the *other* spices.

LILY. 'S'only a packet of mixed spice—

MR. CAUSEWAY. – Some people don't even notice the sweetness in a ginger cake but it's in there.

LILY. Four ounces to be exact.

MR. CAUSEWAY. They don't realise that the heat makes the sweetness all the more rewarding.

(LILY considers him.)

LILY. Made a real study of cake, haven't you?

MR. CAUSEWAY. Yes, I have.

LILY. I'm not a fan of overly sweet things.

MR. CAUSEWAY. Me neither.

(MR. CAUSEWAY loosens his collar after LILY has left and entered the call room. SYLVIE and JANICE enter at the same time.)

LILY. *(to SYLVIE)* Alright now?

JANICE. Yes, thank you.

LILY. I wasn't winding you up, but I think you should be more realistic, you know, in your expectations.

SYLVIE. Thank you, but I don't need advice from you. I am very fine.

LILY. Pardon moi. Well at least we know where we stand *today*, 'cos when you're not on cloud nine you're either crying or kicking the cat—

TIFFANY. – What cat?

SYLVIE. You are a ridiculous old woman.

JANICE. Try not to get wound up, Sylvie.

LILY. It's a pain having to tiptoe around her.

JANICE. I don't see much tip-toeing coming/[from you]—

LILY. – There's a layer of eggshells round her so wide they go out the door, up the stairs and onto the street. Eggs! Oh heck, I've put me foot in it again, *(to SYLVIE)* sorry. Course, we've got to listen to you talk endlessly about oeufs, as you call them.

SYLVIE. *(to LILY)* And your life is full of roses—

LILY. Incubated, propagated, boiled, scrambled, fried. Tiffany has hers over-easy don't you love?

TIFFANY. What? No, I like 'em boiled.

SYLVIE. You understand nothing, you have no compassion for anyone, you talk about your husband like he was a pig—

LILY. He is a pig.

SYLVIE. What about your son, what about him? He rings you once a year on your birthday, you ring him once a year on his birthday, is that what you call a relationship?

LILY. Wakey, wakey. That's called life!

SYLVIE. I think it's sad, I think you are sad.

> (**JANICE** *and* **TIFFANY** *lie low.* **MR. CAUSEWAY** *pokes his head out of the hatch.*)

MR. CAUSEWAY. Now, now, ladies, can the heated debates take place outside of work hours, please? *(Getting softer)* Please... Please...

LILY. *(sotto voce)* When you do get a kiddie, your relationship's going to be perfect of course.

SYLVIE. I would need a bad brain to make it worse than yours.

LILY. Well good luck with that one, madam.

(Long awkward pause. Tense atmosphere in the room.)

TIFFANY. *(unaware of the gravity)* It's mental, really, when you think that some women died having kids, and others died trying to get rid of 'em.

(Silence)

(Lights out)

(Lights up on:)

Scene Two

*(A new day. **LILY** is in the call room unwrapping a cake at her desk. Next to it is a large birthday card. **MR. CAUSEWAY** enters the call room purposefully but without an actual purpose. He looks over to **LILY** for a reaction.)*

MR. CAUSEWAY. *(singing)* Happy birthday to you.

LILY. Thank you for the card, Mr. C, it's very witty.

MR. CAUSEWAY. I thought you'd like it. *(apropos the card, thinks he's being witty)* **Quack!**

*(**LILY** laughs tactfully. He hangs about, pleased with himself but then does not know what to do.)*

Well those orders won't dispatch themselves.

(He bounds into his office.)

*(**JANICE** rushes in, hot and sweaty. She is bundled down with bags and is wearing a painted pasta necklace)*

JANICE. Almost on bloody time. *(She notices the card.)* Happy birthday, Lily, I'll have to get your card in my break, I just couldn't fit it all in this morning, sorry, love.

LILY. Don't bother, you know I think it's a load of nonsense.

*(**MR. CAUSEWAY** hears and is visibly deflated.)*

JANICE. Oh you'll get one if only to prove I can *do it all* as they say in the mags.

LILY. Like that is it?

JANICE. It would be nice to drink my coffee in peace and at a table *not* covered in Copydex, jam, glitter or hundreds and thousands. *(Looks around her)* Still, no grimy mitts here, eh?

*(**JANICE** pops into **MR. CAUSEWAY**'s office.)*

I'm sorry, Mr. C, Matilda left her school project on the kitchen table and I had to go back home to get it.

MR. CAUSEWAY. *(grumpy)* Hmm.

JANICE. No Sylvie?

MR. CAUSEWAY. *Also late*, as is Tiffany. I'm going to have to mete out some penalties, this can't go on.

(*JANICE exits his office.*)

JANICE. *(whispers)* Someone got out of bed the wrong way.

LILY. He was fine a minute ago.

(*TIFFANY enters, bleary eyed and dishevelled.*)

Good night?

(*TIFFANY shakes her head, chucks her bag on the floor and flops onto her chair, slumps onto her desk and puts her head in her hands without removing her coat.*)

Oh deary me.

(*SYLVIE enters. She is very pale and depressed-looking.*)

Christ, you look worse than she does.

(*SYLVIE wells up and runs to the toilets. JANICE follows her. LILY rolls her eyes heavenward.*)

It's like *Emergency Ward Ten* in here, not that any of you lot will remember that.

(*TIFFANY remains slumped in the desk.*)

(*LILY puts her head set on.*)

(*MR. CAUSEWAY pops his head out of his hatch.*)

MR. CAUSEWAY. *(to LILY)* Lily. Personal call.

(*Spotlight on LILY.*)

LILY. That you, son?… Thank you. How's tricks?… Keeping well?… It's all much of a muchness my end… You've rung early, busy day? *(Awkward pause)*… Yeah, well thanks for calling. Take care… Sorry? *(Long pause)*… *(She puts down her knitting)*… I'm not sure I get you… I never questioned it… Well it does seem to be the trend… It's not a criticism, it's an observation… *Me* being defensive?… Well all I can say is we didn't have all these expectations in my day, we just got on with it. You *all* want more than you can have, and I don't only mean *things*. Everyone thinks they're entitled somehow. I don't know what's going on in people's heads I really don't, I don't know what's going on in **your** head— … What?… Oh! *(Long pause)*… Well what do you suggest?… Stop phoning!… I see. You don't think you're going a bit over-the-top?… Well if this is what you want… Then I suppose this is good/[bye]...

(Call over. **LILY** *sits with her headset on looking bemused. She allows the stitches to fall off her needle.)*

(Lights down on **LILY** *and up on the bathroom.)*

*(***JANICE** *catches sight of herself in the mirror. She grabs at the pasta necklace, throws it in the basin and wipes the paint from her neck.)*

JANICE. *(at the mirror)* Bloody heck, I meant to take this off, look at the state of me *(wiping at the paint on her neck).*

*(***SYLVIE** *emerges from the toilet, composed. She washes her hands.)*

Have you?

*(***SYLVIE** *nods.)*

SYLVIE. I could feel it coming, the pains started in the night, I haven't slept. Arghhh! I guess I have to tell Davide. *(Examines the bags under her eyes)* I cried all night.

JANICE. Oh love.

SYLVIE. We can't afford to try again. If it was up to me we would sell the house but Davide won't. Who needs a house when there are no children? *(Looks in the mirror)* He doesn't have to live with the same sense of failure as me.

JANICE. You're not a failure.

SYLVIE. Yes they all tell you that but that's not what *I* feel—

JANICE. Maybe in time—

SYLVIE. If you want something you go after it, you don't give up halfway. What is money compared to a life?

JANICE. I wish I knew what to say.

SYLVIE. *(gently)* I'm tired, you know, of hating every pregnant woman I see.

*(**SYLVIE** readjusts her make-up.)*

I have to carry on like normal, but inside I want to scream. *(Takes a long look at herself)* I don't like who I've become. That old woman has a point.

JANICE. She does not, don't be daft.

*(**JANICE** gives her a hug. They both check themselves in the mirror. **JANICE** wipes another dab of paint from her neck. **SYLVIE** takes out her mobile and gives **JANICE** a little nod. **JANICE** understands that **SYLVIE** needs some privacy and enters the call room. While dialling, **SYLVIE** casually picks up the necklace and then focuses on it.)*

SYLVIE. Can I speak with mister—

(She chokes up, presses the 'off' button on the phone, drops the necklace back in the basin and runs into the toilet cubicle.)

(Lights off in the bathroom, up in the call room.)

*(**TIFFANY** has fallen asleep at her desk.)*

JANICE. You alright, Lily? You look like you've seen a ghost!… *Lily?*

TIFFANY. Whoa! I wasn't asleep, I was just resting my eyes...

LILY. Hmm?

JANICE. *(to **LILY**)* I said are you alright? You look miles away.

TIFFANY. What? No, I got chucked so I went on a bender. I thought he really like me an' all.

LILY. *(to herself)* Happy bloody birthday.

*(She looks at the lost stitches but does not try and retrieve them; it's as if the task is too big. **JANICE**'s mobile rings.)*

JANICE. *(answering it)* What now?… Oh, I do apologize, Miss McGrath. *(Panic)*… What?… Is he hurt? Where did he fall?… Is he conscious?… *(Annoyed)* I see… Yes, I'm fine, thanks for asking… I can be there in half an hour.

(She ends the call. To **TIFFANY** *and* **LILY***)*

Craig's fallen off the slide. He was trying to get *up* it, the little fucker. The school wants me there. *(Apologetic)* It's a precaution.

*(***JANICE*** collects her things, annoyed.)*

TIFFANY. God! It must be bad. My mum never came for me even when I broke my arm.

JANICE. He's scraped his knee. I've told him a thousand times not to climb. He'll need a bloody hospital when I get hold of him. Someone tell Mr. C. for us.

*(***TIFFANY*** nods. ***JANICE*** exits.)*

*(***SYLVIE*** enters. She is lost in thought.)*

TIFFANY. I need a Red Bull, anyone want anyfin'?

*(***LILY*** and ***SYLVIE*** are too lost in their own thoughts to hear.)*

I'm going out, **do you want anyfin'**?

*(They both ignore her. ***TIFFANY*** shrugs and pops her head in the office doorway.)*

TIFFANY. Mr. C, can I pop out?

MR. CAUSEWAY. You only just got here.

TIFFANY. Cheers.

*(***TIFFANY*** exits.)*

(Plaintive music.)

*(***SYLVIE*** and ***LILY*** are alone; each is contemplating her own sadness.)*

*(What happens next is like a series of tableaux or a very slow dance. This may be performed to music, ***LILY*** and ***SYLVIE*** go into various positions which are ordinary but when done in unison seem a little surreal. The lighting should reflect this.)*

(They sit facing forward for half a minute or so. They both stand up and face each other, one going to get a

drink and the other getting something out of the pocket of her coat. They sit back down, then they both find items to put into their handbags. For **LILY** *it is a spare ball of wool and for* **SYLVIE** *it is her diary. Then* **SYLVIE** *stands, goes to the kettle and tidies the countertop while waiting for the kettle to boil.* **LILY** *tidies her section. They both rub at something sticky or at a stubborn stain at the same time. When that is done they wait. Or, we could see them perform these actions separately.* **LILY** *wiping away the stain (could be on her dress),* **SYLVIE** *making a drink, then swapping roles. Eventually they should be sitting at opposite ends of the room and facing in opposite directions.)*

(Lights fade.)
(Lights up on:)

Scene Three

(A new day. **LILY** *is taking a call,* **SYLVIE** *and* **JANICE** *are processing orders.* **MR. CAUSEWAY** *is in his office.* **LILY** *is unusually impatient with the caller, which does not go unnoticed by the others.)*

LILY. You could buy her a pair of nipple clamps or for seventeen ninety-five, the bumper set of Tit Tweakers. You'll see them on page five… Well then what about the Bongo-Bongo Tradesman's Entrance Dildo?… All of our leather goods are black…they come in small, medium, and liar, the codpiece comes in extra large, porky… *(Impatient)* Less expensive? Right. Anal jelly – the glitter version, now that's very celebratory and quite a lot cheaper. *(Sighs)… Right then*, the avocado shaped love-egg… Wait one sec, *(shouts out to no-one in particular)* Would you say the avocado love-egg is the same size as a 'Hass'?… Yes it is, everyone agrees it's roughly that size—

*(***MR. CAUSEWAY*** *pops his head out of the hatch.)*

MR. CAUSEWAY. Lily.

LILY. Why not browse the catalogue *before* calling next time? I haven't got all bloody day.

*(***MR. CAUSEWAY*** *steps out of his office.)*

MR. CAUSEWAY. *(coughs)* Could I have a word, Lillian?

(They both exit the call room and enter the office.)

(Lights focus on **SYLVIE** *and* **JANICE**.*)*

SYLVIE. Davide has started the adoption process.

JANICE. That's good, isn't it?

SYLVIE. Yes, I put down my signature.

JANICE. But?

SYLVIE. It's the sensible thing to do, I know.

JANICE. Yes.

SYLVIE. He doesn't want to see me go through any more heartbreak.

JANICE. *(agrees)* No.

SYLVIE. I can't accept that I'll never… Janice, my heart is going to break.

JANICE. Come here, come on.

(**JANICE** *embraces* **SYLVIE**.)

Sylvie, I'm going to say something now, please try not to take it the wrong way. *(Pause)* Do you want a baby or do you want to be pregnant?

SYLVIE. What?

(**SYLVIE** *moves away.*)

JANICE. I just meant—

SYLVIE. Is there something wrong with wanting to be pregnant?

JANICE. Maybe pregnancy is not the be-all you think it is.

SYLVIE. I don't want to go through the motions of being a mother. I want to feel it—

JANICE. You would still be a mother—

SYLVIE. I want to have *my* baby, I want to see what kind of baby *we* make. I don't want to get to know a stranger.

JANICE. But what more you can do?

SYLVIE. *(defiant)* I'll find a way.

(*Lights down on* **SYLVIE** *and* **JANICE** *and up on the office.*)

MR. CAUSEWAY. Is everything alright?

LILY. I couldn't manage it today.

MR. CAUSEWAY. I've noticed that you've not been yourself of late—

LILY. It didn't work out.

MR. CAUSEWAY. Not bad news or anything?

LILY. It was terrible.

MR. CAUSEWAY. Oh my dear Lilian, I'd like to think that you can tell me.

LILY. I'm not used to failure, you know, in *that* way.

MR. CAUSEWAY. We are all of us fallible—

LILY. I'm that, alright.

MR. CAUSEWAY. If there's anything I can do, anything at all?

(*She looks at him quizzically.*)

LILY. It's good of you to offer, but what on earth could *you* do?

MR. CAUSEWAY. Oh my goodness, it is bad—

LILY. Only really fit for the bin.

MR. CAUSEWAY. Sorry?

LILY. I had to *scrape* it out of the tin.

MR. CAUSEWAY. Are you talking about your cake?

(*She looks at him, puzzled for a second, then slumps onto the chair.*)

LILY. I used to have everything all worked out.

MR. CAUSEWAY. *Now* I'm worried.

LILY. Me too.

MR. CAUSEWAY. No! I'm worried about *you*—

LILY. It's like people—

MR. CAUSEWAY. What?

LILY. You can't *really* know them—

MR. CAUSEWAY. I'm confused—

LILY. I mean, take me, what can you tell about me?

(**MR. CAUSEWAY** *clears his throat.*)

MR. CAUSEWAY. Well I've had the privilege of knowing you for some years and—

LILY. It's a waste of time trying.

MR. CAUSEWAY. I'm a good judge of character and/[like to think]—

LILY. I mean you think you know someone—

MR. CAUSEWAY. Can see beyond the/[exterior]—

LILY. (*hardening*) – So we're not the closest mother and son that ever lived. Is that a reason to sever all ties?

(**MR. CAUSEWAY** *almost takes her hand but stops himself.*)

I was a good mother. He never wanted for anything, always nicely turned out, clothes cleaned, pressed, *and* he was well fed.

MR. CAUSEWAY. I'm sure—

(**LILY** *stands.*)

LILY. If he doesn't want to talk, fine, it won't kill me.

(**MR. CAUSEWAY** *looks lost.* **LILY** *exits his office and enters the call room.*)

(**SYLVIE** *and* **JANICE** *stop talking abruptly when* **LILY** *enters.* **SYLVIE** *and* **JANICE** *stare at* **LILY** *and she at them: it's a momentary stand-off.*)

(*Lights out.*)

(*Lights up on:*)

Scene Four

(A new day, early morning. **MR. CAUSEWAY** *is bent over his paperwork in his office.* **SYLVIE** *is in the call room, agitated and desperate, talking into her mobile.)*

(The board states that this is July.)

SYLVIE. This is *very* inconvenient and I'm sure he won't be happy with this service either.

(She clicks off and paces. **JANICE** *enters.)*

JANICE. God! Am I on time?

SYLVIE. *(urgent)* Janice! You can help me.

JANICE. What's up?

(She struggles with her coat and bags until **SYLVIE** *almost rips them off her.)*

SYLVIE. I need Jim to pretend to be Davide, just for a phone call.

JANICE. What? No, why?

SYLVIE. Wait! I just called the bank manager to extend our loan. But he wants Davide to confirm it so I'll say, 'I have Davide right here but he is very busy', I told him that already. Jim says 'yes we would like to add four thousand pounds to the loan' and that's it, I've done it before with Davide, twice, it's always the same.

JANICE. Lie?

SYLVIE. I will pay the money back – anyway I don't care.

JANICE. Don't you think you're getting in a bit over your head here?

SYLVIE. It does not matter.

(Mr. C. pokes his head out of the hatch.)

MR. CAUSEWAY. Call on line one.

*(***JANICE** *goes for the phone.* **SYLVIE** *stops her.)*

JANICE. But how are you going to explain it?

SYLVIE. *Look!* A stupid little clerk just makes a check that he has ticked every little box, it's a formality. I can't wait, my time is now.

MR. CAUSEWAY. No one free?

JANICE. David's going to notice a four thousand pound increase, and then there's the interest – that'll accrue—

SYLVIE. I don't want to debate, I don't want to make a justice.

MR. CAUSEWAY. No? I'll take it then, shall I?

JANICE. It's not right, Sylvie.

SYLVIE. I'm not trying to *steal* it. Please, ask him.

MR. CAUSEWAY. Fine, I'm taking it.

JANICE. I'm very sorry.

SYLVIE. *(quietly pleading)* Please, don't say no, it's just a phone call. I don't want to ask Davide.

JANICE. *(also soft)* Because he won't approve.

SYLVIE. *(getting wound up)* Since when do you think of that? I don't care if he agrees. This is my last chance. What will my life be if I don't take it? I have to live with myself—

JANICE. You might always feel like you've got one more chance—

SYLVIE. I'm thirty-nine. I don't have enough eggs left. They have made it clear.

(They look at each other in silence, the significance clear.)

So I'm begging you, Janice, please, just ask him.

*(**JANICE** reluctantly picks up her mobile.)*

JANICE. I know the answer. *(She dials)* Jim?… *(Flat)* Yeah, everything's fine, love… What? No. It *is*, honestly… I know!… Yeah it is a bloody miracle… Now you ask, no, I never went back for anything, you? *(Laughs)* Oh what are we like… Look, I just rang to *(looks at* **SYLVIE** *then looks away)*… I thought – I'm calling to say… *(she surprises herself)* Hello!… We should… That would be lovely, strange, but lovely… I love you too. *(She ends the call.)* Gosh, that was a bit surreal. I'm sorry, Sylvie, I know I didn't ask, I couldn't.

SYLVIE. *(angry)* No, obviously … I thought I could count on you, but I can see that I am completely alone in this, I've got no one.

JANICE. I'm sorry you feel alone. I wish I could help. If there was another way, I would.

SYLVIE. Ha! Another way, another time, anything else, Sylvie, but not this.

JANICE. Hold on a minute, I think this is crossing a line, you're going too far, you really are.

SYLVIE. *(fierce) How*? How have I gone too far? Too far for you? I haven't gone far enough.

JANICE. You wanted Jim to lie.

SYLVIE. So what? People lie every day. No one is dying.

JANICE. *(angry)* I'm pretty sure it's fraud then and that would carry a potential jail sentence!

SYLVIE. Fraud! Pah! You are so dramatic.

JANICE. That's a laugh coming from *you*. I *have* supported you. I think I've been very supportive. I'm just not going to do what you want or ask my husband to. You're losing your grip.

*(****SYLVIE**** forcefully throws her Mothercare catalogue into the bin just as **MR. CAUSEWAY** enters the room. He is startled. **JANICE** and **SYLVIE** halt their conversation while he picks up some papers from the returns table and goes back to his office.)*

SYLVIE. Why did I expect you to understand? You with five children, you are going to tell me when to give up trying for *one*. Why did you want so many? You're not even a Catholic—!

JANICE. You can't think further than the pregnancy. You've got no bloody idea what it's like. I'm in a permanent state of anxiety, worrying if they're healthy. Are they being bullied? Will they bully? Why aren't Matilda's legs straight? Will it affect her self esteem? Will she get a boyfriend? Is Lee *ever* going to make a friend—

SYLVIE. Yes you complain all the time, about the effort they are, that you have no time for yourself, to even take a shit in peace! Why did you have more if you felt like that—?

JANICE. I didn't know did I? I mean you get them over one stage and there's another bloody stage to take its place. And always in the back of my mind: how are they going to turn out? How will *I* make them turn out? Will they be selfish bastards? Will they fit into society or not contribute to it in any way whatsoever—

SYLVIE. Still, you can't wait to come *here*.

(Indicates the room)

JANICE. So I need to get away? Resent them even? God, why am I justifying this? It's not like I'm not thinking of them constantly, about things that are there, and everything that's not. The weight of responsibility is overwhelming. *I am nothing <u>but</u> a mother…* If Jim wasn't there to remind me who I used to be I'd wonder if the old Janice ever existed… I find myself imagining how he'd cope if I left. I wouldn't, but if *I'm* thinking that, what's *he* thinking? D'you know, I'm halfway through a book I started in two thousand and ten—!

SYLVIE. You should try ONLY having this, *only* yourself to think about, it's terrifying!

*(They look at each other. **JANICE** softens.)*

JANICE. I know.

SYLVIE. You don't wish you didn't have them.

*(**JANICE** shakes her head at the thought.)*

JANICE. If anything happened to one of them…

SYLVIE. I want to care that much.

JANICE. I know. I feel ashamed. When I look at Tiff and I see how carefree she is…and you, always so smartly/ [dressed]—

(TIFFANY enters, full of beans.)

TIFFANY. *(excited)* Oh, my, God, I had the best time, Georgio was sooo sweet, he was all over me. But, right, he's got this mattress called a Tampa or something and it's really springy so when I was on top we just kept bouncing up and down in the same direction and my legs got really tired and he couldn't get—

JANICE. *(flat)* We need milk.

TIFFANY. Off… What? Oh, you want me to go and—?

JANICE. You've got your coat on.

TIFFANY. Right, yeah, I'll just be a tick.

(She goes to leave.)

TIFFANY. Is everything alright?

SYLVIE. No.

JANICE. No.

(TIFFANY exits, pronto. There is a pause, SYLVIE retrieves the Mothercare catalogue.)

JANICE. Did I ever tell you about when I was a P.A.?

SYLVIE. Quite a few times.

JANICE. *(laughs gently)* Yeah, I look back and laugh about how stressed I got back then and over what? But I did love it. *(Long pause)* There are other things you can do with your life that are worthwhile, if, you know—

SYLVIE. Like inventing the cure for cancer?

JANICE. No, I meant *really* worthwhile.

(SYLVIE looks perplexed, then they both smile.)

I've painted a terrible picture of motherhood.

SYLVIE. It doesn't look like a terrible picture to me. *(Pause)*

JANICE. I'm sorry, sorry that I can't ask Jim to—

SYLVIE. I shouldn't have asked, I know that.

(MR. CAUSEWAY checks from his hatch that the coast is clear and enters the call room.)

MR. CAUSEWAY. Where's Tiffany? She was just here.

(Janice and Sylvie don't answer.)

MR. CAUSEWAY. And *still* no Lily? Has she rung anyone?

JANICE. She's gone to get milk.

MR. CAUSEWAY. Lily?

JANICE. No, Tiff.

MR. CAUSEWAY. Oh, I see… Hang on, *more* milk? We'll be drowning in it, I bought two litres yesterday. Is someone stealing it? Sylvie doesn't even drink the stuff. How are four of us going to get through it all? If Lillian doesn't come to work that's three of us. I can count on one hand the number of days that woman has had off.

JANICE. You seem very agitated, Mr. C, maybe Lily's just late.

MR. CAUSEWAY. She's never late.

*(**TIFFANY** enters with milk. **MR. CAUSEWAY** turns on her.)*

I suppose it's skimmed?

*(**TIFFANY** nearly jumps out of her skin at his reaction when he sees that it is skimmed.)*

Oh perfect, we can't freeze it, skimmed milk doesn't freeze, it's to do with the fat content. Well theoretically you can but it needs to be in small quantities because it takes a long time to thaw out. And when it is finally defrosted you have to shake it vigorously to ensure the milk is blended because it separates during freezing and goes watery after thawing. She should have a mobile.

JANICE. I'll take it home, we can always use it.

SYLVIE. She has one but I've never seen her use it, I don't think she knows how.

MR. CAUSEWAY. Of course she knows how, she obviously chooses not to. It can't come out of the kitty, the books still have to balance, we can't have/[the company]—

SYLVIE. – I'll buy the milk, for Janice.

*(**SYLVIE** gets her purse.)*

JANICE. Thank you, Sylvie.

MR. CAUSEWAY. I don't need this kind of stress, I really don't. I'll be in my office.

TIFFANY. Do you want a cup of tea, Mr. C?

MR. CAUSEWAY. NO!

(Enters his office then comes back out.)

Er sorry…yes, please, Tiffany, thank you.

(Lights out.)

(Lights up on:)

Scene Five

(A new day)

*(**MR. CAUSEWAY** hovers near the door of the call room. **SYLVIE** enters.)*

MR. CAUSEWAY. She rang in, she's been at the hospital.

SYLVIE. *(not bothered)* Oh.

MR. CAUSEWAY. Yes, well.

(He exits the call room and enters his office.)

*(**JANICE** enters the call room. **MR. CAUSEWAY** pops his head out of his office door.)*

I was just telling Sylvie, Lillian has been at the hospital all night.

JANICE. My God, is she alright?

MR. CAUSEWAY. Haha, yes, she's fine… *(Coughs)* Oh, yes, it's Bill.

JANICE. What's the matter with him?

MR. CAUSEWAY. *(completely unconcerned)* No idea.

(He enters his office.)

JANICE. How are you? How did it go?

SYLVIE. We are on the list. Like the woman said, 'all systems go'.

JANICE. And?

SYLVIE. I lied, even Davide believed me. I should become an actress. He doesn't suspect, so he won't ask questions. *(She rubs the empty finger)* If I sell my mother's jewellery at an auction house I'll just have enough, I took it this morning. Now I wait.

JANICE. And if a baby is offered to you?

SYLVIE. After…this try, you know. If it doesn't happen, I guess… I don't know—

*(**SYLVIE**'s mobile rings. She answers and walks upstage. We don't hear her conversation.)*

*(**TIFFANY** enters carrying a posh little carrier bag. **MR. CAUSEWAY** pops his head out of the hatch.)*

MR. CAUSEWAY. Ten minutes late, Tiffers.

*(**TIFFANY** gives **JANICE** a quizzical look.)*

TIFFANY. *(mouths the word)* Tiffers? *(Out loud)* Sorry.

JANICE. He's all over the shop. Lily's husband isn't well.

TIFFANY. Oh, poor Lil. And Bill, poor Bill, what's wrong with him?

JANICE. I don't know… What have you got in the fancy bag?

TIFFANY. I bought these really amazing cufflinks for my new man, do you want to see?

JANICE. God, how long have you known him?

TIFFANY. I saw him five times last week. Anyway, they said I can take them back if he doesn't like them. They were only a hundred and twenty.

JANICE. *(sarcastic)* Oh he'll like them.

(She shows them.)

TIFFANY. Yeah.

JANICE. How old are you, Tiffany?

TIFFANY. Twenty-nine.

JANICE. My God, I had three kids by the time I was your age.

TIFFANY. No way.

JANICE. Still at least someone's got disposable income. Is he *the one*?

TIFFANY. Dunno.

SYLVIE. *(shouts)* Putain j'y crois pas! *(Translates – "I can't believe it!")*

TIFFANY. What?

*(**SYLVIE** bangs her phone in disgust.)*

SYLVIE. I have to wait three months for the auction, it's too long.

TIFFANY. I thought someone had died.

SYLVIE. *(to* JANICE*)* Don't say anything.

(She flops down in her chair, defeated. TIFFANY *is curious.)*

JANICE. Sell it somewhere else.

SYLVIE. I wouldn't get enough, I tried.

JANICE. Perhaps the clinic can defer payment.

TIFFANY. What's that?

SYLVIE. Ha! Can you imagine. If it failed, no one would pay, *ever*.

TIFFANY. Pay what?

SYLVIE. Oh God, one minute there is hope, the next…

TIFFANY. What?

(They both look at her.)

I was just trying to help, but if you don't wanna tell me.

SYLVIE. 'Ow can you help, huh?

TIFFANY. Sorr-ee.

(Tense atmosphere in the room)

(Feeling clever) Is it about a baby?

SYLVIE. HA! You guessed, you're brilliant! You should become a detective *(to herself)* except that it's always about that. I can't remember the last time I thought of anything else.

TIFFANY. I thought—

SYLVIE. Even asleep there is no escape. You know what I dreamt last night? That I had a baby boy. He was about two years old, he had soft red hair, parted like this. *Me*, I had him. I felt it and it was so real. When I woke up I still believed he was mine, and I loved him so much. For a full ten minutes. When I realised it was a dream, I could still feel the love, and then I felt the loss… *(Pause, soft) Really,* for a whole ten minutes. *(Pause)* It's not possible for me to switch off, there is no peace.

(Pause)

TIFFANY. I thought it was about something else. I thought you was going on about money – or something.

JANICE. Why, have you got some? I guess you have if you can afford to buy trinkets!

TIFFANY. No I haven't, I always ask Lily, she lent me for these.

(She holds out the cufflinks.)

JANICE. You ask Lily? Not your parents or a friend?

TIFFANY. She don't judge, you know—

SYLVIE. *(light bulb moment)* Really?

JANICE. *(to* **SYLVIE***)* You're joking.

TIFFANY. No-oo, I mean she takes the piss and that but she does that anyway.

SYLVIE. Yes! Why not?

JANICE. You can't stand her!

SYLVIE. It's not important.

JANICE. She *likes* her. She'd never lend it to *you.*

TIFFANY. She ain't got nothing to spend it on.

SYLVIE. Would she have four thousand pounds?

*(***TIFFANY*** shrugs a 'don't know'. ***SYLVIE*** stands up.)*

Where is she?

JANICE. At the hospital. Bill is ill, remember?

SYLVIE. *(to* **TIFFANY***)* When will she be back? You can phone her.

JANICE. And say what, exactly?

TIFFANY. I got my phone nicked and everyone's numbers is all gone.

*(***SYLVIE*** considers. She knocks on ***MR. CAUSEWAY****'s door.)*

MR. CAUSEWAY. Come.

SYLVIE. So, what did Lily say?

MR. CAUSEWAY. Oh, I thought you were offering tea—

SYLVIE. Tiffany, you were making the tea.

TIFFANY. Was I?

SYLVIE. So?

MR. CAUSEWAY. Sorry? Oh yes. She telephoned to say that she spent the day at the hospital with her hus—

SYLVIE. When is she back?

MR. CAUSEWAY. I don't know, I'm sure she wouldn't take time off if it wasn't/[serious]—

SYLVIE. Eh merde. How can we find out?

MR. CAUSEWAY. I didn't think you—

SYLVIE. I'd like to know she is alright, have you got her number?

MR. CAUSEWAY. Yes but I can't go handing it out without her consent, I mean if she hasn't given it to you herself—

SYLVIE. – Fine! No worries.

(She goes to leave his office barely hiding her annoyance then changes her mind and demeanour.)

Please, just tell her that we are all thinking of her at this difficult time. You will be speaking to her soon?

MR. CAUSEWAY. I was going to wait for her to call in, I didn't want to burden her.

SYLVIE. Really?

MR. CAUSEWAY. Why? Do you think I should—?

SYLVIE. I think it would be good for her to know we are here for her.

MR. CAUSEWAY. Yes, you are probably right. Thank you Sylvie, I shall. *(Expecting her to leave)*

SYLVIE. When?

MR. CAUSEWAY. What?

SYLVIE. When will you phone?

MR. CAUSEWAY. Err, now?

SYLVIE. It's a good idea, I will leave you to make the call.

*(She waits until he picks up the phone then exits the office. She avoids **JANICE**'s gaze.)*

JANICE. Dear God, I think you've just sunk to a new low.

TIFFANY. How come?

SYLVIE & JANICE. Nothing.

(Lights out)

(Lights up on:)

Scene Six

(A new day)

*(***MR. CAUSEWAY*** *is in his office, working.* ***SYLVIE*** *is in the bathroom looking at herself in the mirror. She looks alone, anxious. She hears someone coming. She freezes for a few seconds.* ***MR. CAUSEWAY*** *hears it too. They both enter the call room expectantly, trying to appear casual. When* ***MR. CAUSEWAY*** *sees* ***JANICE*** *enter, he returns to his office, disinterested.)*

JANICE. *(to* **SYLVIE***)* You're early.

MR. CAUSEWAY. *(without turning round)* You're late.

*(***SYLVIE*** *looks pale and sick.)*

JANICE. She coming in then?

MR. CAUSEWAY. *(offstage)* Yes.

SYLVIE. How I'm going to ask her? I don't think I can.

JANICE. I'm not surprised.

*(***SYLVIE*** *takes a photo out of an official-looking binder in her bag. She shows* **JANICE***.)*

So a baby's come up then?

SYLVIE. Someone *else's* baby.

(She throws it on her desk.)

He wants to spend the weekend choosing the paint for the room and buying a baby bed.

JANICE. Don't you think you ought to at least con[sider]—?

SYLVIE. – No!

(There is someone at the door.)

JANICE. Good luck then.

SYLVIE. Oh God.

*(***MR. CAUSEWAY*** *enters the call room, expectantly. When* ***LILY*** *enters she sees three staring faces. She is taken aback but disguises it.)*

LILY. The three wise monkeys.

(**LILY** *unbuttons her coat.*)

MR. CAUSEWAY. We were worried about you.

SYLVIE. *(a little too quickly)* Yes we were.

LILY. It wasn't me who was ill.

JANICE. How is he?

LILY. Dead.

(*The others are shocked by the bluntness of the statement.*)

MR. CAUSEWAY. I'm very sorry, Lillian.

SYLVIE. Yes I'm very sorry.

(**SYLVIE** *sinks into a chair as though she were the bereaved one.*)

JANICE. You sure you should be here, Lily?

MR. CAUSEWAY. Would you like to sit in my office?

(**LILY** *shrugs a 'don't know'.*)

JANICE. What did he die of?

LILY. Death.

(*No one laughs.*)

Heart attack, three in a row, they come like buses, they brought him back, then he died of complications. They want to do an autopsy. Dunno why, not as if he could leave *his* body to medical science. One thing I did ask, is for them to tell me if he really had a bad back. They won't of course.

(**TIFFANY** *enters.*)

TIFFANY. Hiya, Lily, you're back! How's Bill?

LILY. He died, love. I just came to tell/[you all]—

TIFFANY. *(takes* **LILY***'s hand)* – Oh, poor Lily. Did you get a chance to say goodbye?

LILY. I had days.

TIFFANY. Aww, was it beautiful?

LILY. I never said it, I never said anything. He was afraid an' all. I'd never seen him afraid before. We had bloody hours alone together without a single distraction. No telly for him, no kitchen for me. He said, 'we've had an alright marriage, haven't we, Lil?' I evaded the question. 'At least we went the distance, not like most', fake laugh. I still didn't say anything. 'You weren't too unhappy were you?' … I ask you! That meant he knew, the bastard. I wanted to say, 'You've had years to ask me that, it's too late *now*, you pillock.' What *was* that? Conscience? Fear? God I hated him in that moment. I think he wanted me to take his hand, comfort him. I should have, I know that, I know I should have but I didn't, I couldn't. I was the same with him as I've always been.

MR. CAUSEWAY. That's you all over, Lillian.

LILY. Don't get me wrong, I *used* to want something more, in the early years. I would have liked a *bit* of romance or something bordering on loving but neither of us knew how to get it. And after thirty-six years of, whatever it was we had, you can't just conjure up affection. I didn't feel any. I wanted to feed the ducks if you must know, escape. There was just too much emotion… I did feel sorry for him, but only in the way you feel for a dog that's been mistreated. I thought, why is it you lying there, needy, dying and wanting *something else* from me. Why isn't it the other way round? But if it had been me lay dying, I don't think I would have wanted him anywhere near me.

TIFFANY. Oh, Lils.

LILY. Is this how my Alan is going to feel about me?

TIFFANY. No, of course not, he loves you.

(**LILY** *touches* **TIFFANY**.)

LILY. *(sorrowful)* Your ability to only see the good is what I find charming about you, but I can't help feeling it's going to bite you on the arse some day.

TIFFANY. Really?

MR. CAUSEWAY. Yes, really. Now come on everyone, back to work. As you know, I don't allow alcohol in the workplace, but I think you need a brandy.

LILY. If it's all the same to you I think I'll be on my way. I'm not sure why I came.

(**LILY** *buttons her coat up.*)

SYLVIE. *(to* **JANICE***)* How can I ask now?

(**JANICE** *turns away.*)

SYLVIE. *(stiff)* If you need any help with anything… You will be arranging the funeral, non? So, you know…if I can do anything.

(**LILY** *registers the offer, half bemused but pre-occupied.*)

LILY. I'll see you all in a couple of days I expect. Sorry and all that.

JANICE. Don't be sorry.

(**TIFFANY** *goes after* **LILY** *and touches her.*)

LILY. I'm alright, love.

(**LILY** *exits.*)

MR. CAUSEWAY. C'mon, customers on line one and two.

(**TIFFANY** *and* **JANICE** *answer unenthusiastically.*)

TIFFANY & JANICE. Aphrodite, goddess of sexual rapture.

TIFFANY. The Prik Stick is the most popular—

JANICE. A bicycle pump *or* a foot-pump will do it love—

(**SYLVIE** *is annoyed. She fishes around in her handbag. She takes out her diary. The picture of the prospective baby (the one we have seen before) falls out. She picks it up and looks at it. She screws it up angrily and throws it across the room.*)

(*Lights fade slowly.*)

(*Interval, if one is required*)

(*Lights up on:*)

ACT TWO

Scene One

(A new day. There is a mountain of boxes upstage that have S&TT labels on them.)

*(**MR. CAUSEWAY** has asked **LILY** to come in early, ostensibly to help catch up with a backlog of work. They can either sort through the S&TT boxes or they form a production line behind the returns table. Mr Causeway takes a large rubber/latex bottom from a box and puts it onto the table. With designated sticks, they measure the depth of the anus and the vagina to check that it meets requirements before packing it up ready for dispatch. (They continue doing this task with more bottoms until the end of their conversation.)*

MR. CAUSEWAY. Did they find out what he died of in the end?

LILY. No. Shocking waste of everyone's time. Still, the funeral's Monday, it'll all be done and dusted by then.

MR. CAUSEWAY. Would you like me to come?

LILY. My neighbour Maud's keeping me company.

*(**MR. CAUSEWAY** builds up to asking the next question.)*

MR. CAUSEWAY. Do you believe, that we, go on?

LILY. I fucking hope not 'cos I doubt I'll be going up.

MR. CAUSEWAY. But you're a very good woman.

LILY. My son doesn't seem to think so.

MR. CAUSEWAY. Then he doesn't understand you.

LILY. And I don't understand him, apparently.

MR. CAUSEWAY. Don't put yourself down.

LILY. He said I don't know him, that I'd never known him.

MR. CAUSEWAY. People talk about being understood a lot. *(Pause)* It never ceases to amaze me why they care so much.

LILY. Have you noticed how there's no more cooks these days, only chefs?

MR. CAUSEWAY. Is it the desire to be noticed?

LILY. You can't be a baker, you got to be a *master* baker.

MR. CAUSEWAY. I think of myself as a mere blip put on this earth for a short while, just making up the numbers.

LILY. God only knows what name they're dreaming up for bus drivers! No one's content being average. Actually no one's content full stop.

MR. CAUSEWAY. We are just part of the cycle of life, we are nobodies.

LILY. If you're born with a flat chest you want a big one, on the NHS mind, *(puts on an affected voice)* 'it's affecting my self esteem'.

MR. CAUSEWAY. Too true.

LILY. Maybe that's why there's a need to feel special.

MR. CAUSEWAY. H'mmm. What?

LILY. I mean if it's all a load of nothing, if we *are* just making up the numbers, then it's all a bit pointless really, so—

MR. CAUSEWAY & LILY. What's the point of living?

(They contemplate this for a long pause.)

MR. CAUSEWAY. Do you think you could be depressed?

(She looks at him.)

LILY. If I am, I've been depressed my whole life.

MR. CAUSEWAY. You mustn't let this thing with Alan get to you.

LILY. I don't know where he lives, I think he moved.

MR. CAUSEWAY. Is that a problem?

LILY. I don't know.

MR. CAUSEWAY. I'm sure lots of parents of grown up—

LILY. He used to be in printing, but I couldn't say for definite.

MR. CAUSEWAY. Perhaps things haven't worked out for him like he hoped and he needs someone to blame.

LILY. And who better to blame than your mother, eh?

MR. CAUSEWAY. H'mmm.

LILY. He could be married for all I know. I didn't like to ask, it seemed a bit, intimate. Sounds daft saying that out loud.

MR. CAUSEWAY. There's no law says we should like our relatives.

(**LILY** *is taken aback.*)

LILY. You think I don't like him?

MR. CAUSEWAY. – I didn't say— (that)

LILY. – I couldn't tell you. *(Pause)* Has he got a point d'you think?

MR. CAUSEWAY. I meant you don't *choose* your relatives.

LILY. He didn't *choose* his mother, neither.

MR. CAUSEWAY. No, I suppose— (not)

LILY. – If it's a question of choice, I can choose to know him… But what if I don't like him?

MR. CAUSEWAY. If you don't like him then you won't want to know him, and it won't matter.

LILY. Won't it?

MR. CAUSEWAY. Well, not if—

(Her mind is made up.)

LILY. – I've got a bloody good reason to call him now. That old bastard finally did me a favour.

MR. CAUSEWAY. Alan?

LILY. Bill. Give us a line, will you?

(**LILY** *downs tools and goes to her desk.* **MR. CAUSEWAY** *throws a switch in his office but returns to the call room* *and keeps a distant watch.* **LILY** *dials the number and waits, suddenly anxious.)*

Hello Alan, it's Mum. I know you said you didn't want, you know... Well, I'm respecting that, but it's important I let you know, your father has passed away... I'm fine. Coping. Coping, what am I saying? It was a bit of a shock... I know you didn't speak for a long time, so, I don't know how you feel, about him, this, me... *(Long pause)* Yeah he *was*... Things are obvious in hindsight... *(Awkward silence)* Well the funeral is on Monday. Next Monday, three o'clock, Saint Augustine's. You remember it don't you?... Oh! *(Pause)* I see... No, no, whatever you think is best... Take care then. Goodbye.

(She is obviously shaken. **MR. CAUSEWAY** *approaches.)*

He says he won't be going to his father's funeral.

MR. CAUSEWAY. Oh.

LILY. *(soft)* Sounded like he meant it. That's quite a thing isn't it? Not to pay your last respects... I gave him all the details, you know, if he changes his mind. I don't think he'll miss it. I mean, that would be quite a thing wouldn't it?...

*(***MR. CAUSEWAY** *ventures towards touching* **LILY**'*s hand in some attempt at comfort but she rallies and he loses his nerve as her show of vulnerability lessens.)*

He's making a point, I bet, but when he's had time to think... I've not brought him up like that. He just needs some time to let things land. It's like that sometimes. He'll be there, I'm sure he will.

*(***SYLVIE** *enters, obviously anxious.* **LILY** *puts on her normal front as though nothing had happened.)*

SYLVIE. Morning.

MR. CAUSEWAY. You're very early.

LILY. Morning.

(He exits the room and enters his office. **SYLVIE** *attempts to get* **LILY**'s *attention but finds it hard to make an approach.)*

SYLVIE. Gosh, they ring early.

*(***LILY** *nods and answers.)*

LILY. Aphroditê.

SYLVIE. How are you?

*(***LILY** *shrugs a 'bearing up'.)*

*(***SYLVIE** *strives to act natural.)*

LILY. Sex And The Titty hen night package?

SYLVIE. Good, that's good. If anyone can cope, it will be you.

LILY. Balloons, g-strings, aprons, dildos, wands and penis-shaped scented candles.

SYLVIE. You're a very strong woman which is a good thing, not like me, always, getting stressed.

LILY. Free delivery on orders over sixty-nine pounds.

SYLVIE. Would you like a coffee, a good one?

*(***LILY** *nods a 'why not'.)*

LILY. 'Til stocks last.

SYLVIE. Yes I really need it today.

*(***SYLVIE** *makes coffee.* **LILY** *looks at the mountain of boxes.)*

LILY. We've got very few left so I wouldn't leave it too long.

SYLVIE. I need a little kick.

LILY. Thanks for calling. *(To* **SYLVIE***)* Are you alright?

SYLVIE. What? Oh, yes.

(Awkward silence that **SYLVIE** *tries to fill.)*

I remember when I brought in the cafetiére for the first time. Everyone said it would be too strong and they liked the instant one. But you were the one who said you would try. You said...er? What doesn't kill me can only me make me stronger. Yes, I remembered that. It was funny. And everyone laughed, do you remember it? *(Lily shrugs – she can't remember it.)* I always thought I would like to be like that, open-minded, try new things.

LILY. You moved country, I don't think you have to worry about that.

SYLVIE. That's true but it wouldn't be good to come here and want everything French would it? But I did try a lot of things I think. Some things are better like, er... you accept the differences in people, how people dress, you know, you wear what you like.

LILY. Not me.

SYLVIE. What?… No, I mean, if you turned your hair red or wear a very short skirt, no one would even notice, but in France—

LILY. If I wore a short skirt I think it might start another one of them riots.

SYLVIE. Oh?

LILY. Your lot would call it a revolution I s'pose.

*(**SYLVIE** looks lost.)*

SYLVIE. Yes, perhaps, I mean no, you're not that bad. No, I don't mean—

*(**SYLVIE** goes back to making coffee.)*

LILY. If you're talking about tolerance, I don't think you're talking about me dear.

*(**SYLVIE** drops an empty cup in the sink.)*

SYLVIE. Eh merde.

*(**MR. CAUSEWAY**'s stands in the doorway of his office.)*

MR. CAUSEWAY. I thought I could smell coffee.

SYLVIE. Yes of course, I forgot to ask. I'll bring it.

*(**SYLVIE** encourages him to go back inside. He pops back out at intervals but every interjection is a set-back for **SYLVIE**.)*

(**LILY** *starts knitting.* **SYLVIE** *tries again with the coffee. She leans against the counter top for support and gathers her courage.*)

I have something to ask you.

(**LILY** *stops knitting and looks at* **SYLVIE**.)

LILY. Oh yes.

SYLVIE. I know that this is not a good time for you, it's the worst time probably… I know as well that you and me, we don't get on really well sometimes.

(**MR. CAUSEWAY** *pops his head out of the hatch.*)

MR. CAUSEWAY. Not going to Brazil to get it are you?

SYLVIE. Just coming. Um... how to say this. I wouldn't ask but—

MR. CAUSEWAY. Or Columbia?

SYLVIE. One minute. *(To* LILY*)* I'm… I've got the chance for a last IVF, I need to borrow four thousand pounds. I'm selling something, it will take about three months before I could return the money, I would pay interest of course.

(*The amount hangs in the air.*)

LILY. You're going at it again?

SYLVIE. I would really like to. *(Embarrassed)* You are my last chance.

LILY. You've spent all of your money?

SYLVIE. Yes, stupid isn't it?

LILY. You know I think you're mad.

(**SYLVIE** *nods.*)

You think you'll have a kid and everything will be sunshine and roses don't you? But there are no guarantees in this life.

SYLVIE. I just had to try. I'm sorry.

(**SYLVIE** *goes back to the counter to make the coffee. We see from the back that she is struggling with the disappointment.*)

LILY. My neighbour, Maud. Nursed, fed and worried about her boy for twenty-six years, like most mums. And do you know? He's only gone and fucked off to New Zealand. Says he's not coming back. She's going to have to pay a small fortune and fly halfway round the world just to see him, and she's a martyr to her arthritis I can tell you. How you going to feel if that happens to you?

(**MR. CAUSEWAY** *pops his head out and sees that* **LILY** *is lost in thought and that* **SYLVIE** *is quietly crying. He retreats.*)

I'd planned on leaving my money to my boy.

(**LILY** *is struck by her own sadness for a moment.*)

I don't suppose he even wants it now.

(**SYLVIE** *turns around, her face wet, she looks at* **LILY** *and sees her vulnerability for the first time.*)

SYLVIE. I am sorry for you.

(**LILY** *instantly snaps out of it and is businesslike. She digs in her bag and pulls out a cheque book.*)

LILY. If it all goes pear-shaped, don't say I didn't warn you.

SYLVIE. What does that mean?

LILY. It means, oh never mind. It means *(writing)* I'm leaving the 'who to' blank so you can fill it in.

(**LILY** *hands her the cheque.* **SYLVIE** *does not know how to express her gratitude. She is overwhelmed.*)

SYLVIE. You are making this possible for me.

(**MR. CAUSEWAY** *pops his head out of the hatch and sees the mood has changed.*)

MR. CAUSEWAY. Guatemala! *(To himself, amused)* Do they even grow coffee in Guatemala?

SYLVIE. Yes! Yes of course, it is coming, straight away. Thank you, Lily, *so much.* Oh God, I am so happy.

LILY. Yes, well, just remember what my mother used to say. Laughing only leads to crying.

SYLVIE. But you always try to make people laugh.

LILY. Yeah, I keep trying to prove her wrong.

(Lights fade.)

(Lights up on:)

Scene Two

(A new day. The stage is in darkness. We hear footsteps on the stairs. The door opens. The light is switched on. **MR. CAUSEWAY** *enters.)*

*(***LILY** *is sitting with her stockinged feet out in front of her on another chair. She is wearing a black coat.)*

(Her black hat is on the desk. Her black shoes are on the floor and are caked in mud. She is asleep.)

*(***MR. CAUSEWAY** *turns on the lights and is startled. She wakes, momentarily lost.)*

MR. CAUSEWAY. Oh! You frightened the bloody life out of me. *(Pause)* Have you been here all night?

LILY. Ow! My back! I must have fallen asleep. *(Pause)* I couldn't face going home.

MR. CAUSEWAY. How was it?

LILY. He didn't come… He said he wouldn't and he didn't.

*(***MR. CAUSEWAY** *touches her, involuntarily.)*

MR. CAUSEWAY. I'm sorry Lillian.

(She shrugs.)

Was the send off, you know, alright though?

LILY. It was tragic if you must know.

MR. CAUSEWAY. I knew I should have come.

LILY. *(tries to joke)* That would have made a giddy four of us. But it wasn't the turn-out that was upsetting. I kept thinking I'd see Alan. It was exhausting, turning round, hoping he might creep in at the back somewhere. Hoping he'd drive up in his car when we got to the cemetery. Presuming he's got a car of course! *(Pause)* The service was pitiful, 'his only son, sadly absent' the vicar said. I wanted the ground to swallow me up. I felt like shouting, 'that bastard in the coffin was nothing to do with me, I just kept him alive with food.' Why was I so embarrassed? I mean it's not like the entire congregation didn't *know* him, even Arpad.

MR. CAUSEWAY. Arpad?

LILY. He came and did his feet at the end. I've got a crick in my neck now.

(She heads to the toilet.)

I must spend a wotsit, I can't remember the last time I went through the whole night without going at least once.

(She disappears into the cubicle.)

*(***MR. CAUSEWAY*** picks up one of her shoes, breaks off the caked mud and drops the mud into the waste bin. He holds it up and looks at it, a small and unexpected impulse makes him take a sniff. He hears the toilet flush and puts it down quickly.)*

(Lights fade)

(Lights up on:)

Scene Three

(A new day. All of the S&TT boxes are gone. The board states that this is August.)

*(**MR. CAUSEWAY** hovers between his office and the call room looking at his watch.)*

*(**SYLVIE** enters with a face like thunder. She hangs her coat up and shakes her umbrella angrily.)*

MR. CAUSEWAY. Ah thank goodness, you know how I dislike answering the phones. In fact I thought you were Lily. I was expecting... Sorry. Where are my manners? Good morning, Sylvie.

SYLVIE. *(ready for war)* Is it?

MR. CAUSEWAY. Oh, I see.

SYLVIE. It's the fucking rain, this country.

MR. CAUSEWAY. I was merely being polite.

SYLVIE. Yes, I would expect that, you are English.

MR. CAUSEWAY. I rather think that it's one of our more acceptable traits.

*(**LILY** enters.)*

SYLVIE. *She* doesn't do it.

LILY. What's that then?

SYLVIE. You're not a liar, you say things like they seem, not like everyone else. *(Puts on a mocking voice)* 'Thank you so much, I do apologize, in the present circumstances, *etcetera*'.

LILY. Who rattled your cage?

*(**SYLVIE** laughs a loud, hollow, forced laugh.)*

SYLVIE. You think you are so funny. You know that?

LILY. How am I funny then?

MR. CAUSEWAY. Now then ladies, there's no need for—

SYLVIE. *(almost spitting)* Your stockings are funny, oh no, they're not stockings, they are, what do you call them, poppy socks, actually they are not funny, they are stupid. You don't fool anyone. We know they are not stockings—

MR. CAUSEWAY. There's no need to get per—

LILY. Oh sorry, I forgot I was in the presence of the French fashion police—

MR. CAUSEWAY. This day has not started at all well.

(He enters his office, but we can see him listening.)

SYLVIE. I don't understand a country that thinks a willy-warmer is sexy. My God, if I saw a man coming to bed in one of those… I would leave him instantly.

LILY. It's called a joke.

SYLVIE. Why don't you knit some…some *shoes*, in your cheap, shiny wool. You think it's eccentric – haha, we are so liberated, we can wear whatever we like, we are not embarrassed to look like fucking *shit*.

LILY. I wondered why you always looked like that?

SYLVIE. Like what?

LILY. Like you can smell shit.

SYLVIE. I don't get that, but don't bother to explain, I don't care. I hate this country.

LILY. It's our sense of humour.

SYLVIE. What is?

LILY. A willy-warmer, it's humour. You know, the bit of you that's missing.

SYLVIE. I'm so sorry that I'm not laughing.

(She crashes about, angrily making the coffee.)

LILY. So, it didn't work then?

*(**SYLVIE** gasps as though she needs air to stay alive.)*

SYLVIE. No it didn't, of course it wouldn't. What made me think I ever had a chance. You should have made a bet when you lent me the money, that it would never work. You were right. So now one of us is happy.

LILY. What makes you think I'm happy about it?

SYLVIE. Because you think I'm sentimental, always crying, grieving. You can't understand why I go through the treatments, the injections, the cost, to me and to my body. You can't imagine that anyone could want anything so badly, that they would do all of that. *You*, with your son who means nothing to you, who you don't see from one year to the next, and when your husband is dying you're glad. *Nothing touches you*, I wish I was like you, that I didn't feel anything, want anything, dream of anything. I wish I was dead.

(**SYLVIE** *is crying now.* **LILY** *turns her face away, trying to hold back tears but failing. Both women cry alone.* **MR. CAUSEWAY** *has heard everything.*)

(Lights slowly fade)

(Lights up on:)

Scene Four

(A new day. The board states that JANICE *has sold the most for the month of October.)*

*(*TIFFANY *and* JANICE *are taking calls.* MR. CAUSEWAY *is in his office.)*

JANICE. The two best ejaculation delay sprays are the M25 or for an extra ninety-nine pence, there's the British Rail... No, we don't test them on animals but what you do in the privacy of your own... oh right.

TIFFANY. *(reading from the catalogue)* Immerse the penis in the bag every night for a week to get amazing results... Yep... yes. Great, so one Percy's grow bag.

*(*LILY *enters tentatively. She's been away for a while.)*

*(*MR. CAUSEWAY *steps out of his office to greet her.* TIFFANY *and* JANICE *acknowledge that she's there.)*

JANICE. That'll be seventeen pounds and fifty pence... Can I have the long number on the front?... And the start date?... The three digit security code... Thank you for your custom.

TIFFANY. You never are?. Wicked. Can I have your card number please, Percy... And the dates?... And the three digit security code on the back?... Have fun, Percy.

MR. CAUSEWAY. Feeling better? You must be if that's what I think it is.

TIFFANY. Hi Lily, how are you?

JANICE. You *look* well.

LILY. I just needed a bit of time off. *(To* MR. CAUSEWAY*)* You've lost weight.

*(*LILY *unwraps one of her homemade cakes.)*

MR. CAUSEWAY. I wouldn't be surprised. Mmm, chocolate fudge cake. Shall I be mother?

LILY. Be my guest.

*(*MR. CAUSEWAY *slices the cake.* JANICE *and* TIFFANY *join them.)*

MR. CAUSEWAY. I'm glad you're feeling better, not only because of the delights you bring.

TIFFANY. I hate saying penis, Lily, tell him.

JANICE. You're in the wrong job. That looks lovely.

LILY. I saw a programme on that. Anorexica it's called, they want control over their lives and they're getting back at their mothers apparently.

TIFFANY. *(to* MR. CAUSEWAY*)* I mean it's not very friendly.

JANICE. It can't be that simple. In any case Mr. C *wants* to eat cake, anorexics don't.

MR. CAUSEWAY. Yes, not much danger of that.

TIFFANY. *(to anyone who'll listen)* If I was to say knob, I think it'd be more natural, d'you know what I mean?

LILY. Not simple, Janice, very complex, but I could see how it would work. I'd be really peed off if I made a nice dinner and the person I made it for wouldn't eat it. I couldn't even say that about Bill.

MR. CAUSEWAY. I can't imagine anyone refusing a dinner cooked by you—

TIFFANY. Well?

LILY. Be a good way of getting to me though, wouldn't it? Mess about with it for ten minutes then leave it on the plate. It's clever when you look at it, no one can accuse you of anything nasty.

TIFFANY. What do you think?

MR. CAUSEWAY. I've told you, Tiffany, it's unprofessional.

*(*TIFFANY *shrugs, dejected.)*

JANICE. *(to* LILY*)* I've sold a hundred and twenty-six vibrators since you've been gone.

LILY. Well the world's a happier place then. How's the kids? How's your love life, Tiff?

JANICE. Trudy got into big school, thank God, we would have had to move house if she hadn't.

TIFFANY. I'm back with Georgio.

LILY. Blimey, that a record?

TIFFANY. Yeah it's mental.

(*They all laugh.*)

LILY. No Sylvie?

JANICE. She's gone to Guatemala to collect that baby girl.

LILY. Really?

MR. CAUSEWAY. Oh yes, she said to give you this.

(**MR. CAUSEWAY** *takes an envelope out of his shirt pocket. He hands it to* **LILY**. **LILY** *steps away and opens the letter. It is full of money and there is a small card.* **LILY** *reads it and is touched by something but keeps it to herself.*)

LILY. Whose putting the tea on, then? I'm spitting feathers here.

MR. CAUSEWAY. What did you do with yourself then?

LILY. Watched telly. Fat people could have a channel to themselves. On *Ten-Ton-Teen*, this nineteen stone kid had a mother that couldn't leave off from feeding him. They told her he'd die but she was still stuffing pizza into him saying, 'you can't eat nothing, son'. He looked like he could do with eating nothing for ten years. Emotional baggage, that is. I never thought people would want to watch that sort of thing, but I suppose it's all about the struggle isn't it?

MR. CAUSEWAY. (*being humorous*) So you've taken a psychology degree and done *some* relaxing I hope.

LILY. Got Sky now. They give you this package to 'suit your viewing *demands*'. That's what they call it. I think I'll introduce it into the patter. Demanding, I ask you.

TIFFANY. Oh you're so funny, Lily.

LILY. You haven't changed I see. Still bounding about, oblivious – and yes, before you ask, yes I mean it in a good way.

TIFFANY. Ha ha, see! She's mad. What else did you watch?

LILY. Remakes of old films and some of the new films but they're about the end of the world mostly, I fell asleep through a lot of them in spite of all the loud explosions. I must have been dog tired. Look at me, I can't stop talking.

MR. CAUSEWAY. It's good to try new things.

LILY. Yeah, Arpad came over and watched some of them with me.

(**MR. CAUSEWAY** *bridles.*)

TIFFANY. I-pad? That's hilarious.

LILY. Arpad, you daft monkey, he's Polish.

MR. CAUSEWAY. Hungarian actually.

LILY. What?

MR. CAUSEWAY. Arpad, it's of Hungarian origin. The name of course, no idea about the chap. He did Bill's feet if I remember correctly. So what? He's a hanger-on now is he?

TIFFANY. Oh I've missed you, Lils.

LILY. I think he just wanted a bit of company. Like me I s'pose. *(Shy)* I've missed you too, all of you.

JANICE. Well I'd better be off, I've got to pick Joe up. It's good to have you back, Lily, I knew I wouldn't stay on my prime spot for long.

(**JANICE** *puts on her coat and exits.*)

(**LILY** *takes* **MR. CAUSEWAY** *to one side.*)

LILY. Can I have a word, Mr. C?

(*They enter his office. He has a cup of tea on the go.*)

(*Lights on the office*)

MR. CAUSEWAY. I think caution is advisable at this delicate time. These are unchartered waters, you are newly liberated, you don't want to do anything rash.

LILY. I'm not following.

MR. CAUSEWAY. *(smarting)* The film buff. Only he may not be thinking about your welfare.

LILY. *(incredulous)* He's only twenty-eight.

MR. CAUSEWAY. Yes, well. *(He coughs)* Even so. *(He gestures to a chair.)*

LILY. Look, you've told me you didn't have a good relationship with *your* mother.

MR. CAUSEWAY. No, I could never please her.

LILY. 'Cos, now I'm wondering. Did I get complacent, should I have expected more? I mean, did you try to change your situation?

(He takes a moment to think.)

MR. CAUSEWAY. I spent years trying to be the kind of son I thought she wanted me to be. But then I came to the conclusion that she was a cold-hearted bitch.

LILY. Is that why you like me?

*(**MR. CAUSEWAY** spits his tea out with great force, it hits the desk.)*

MR. CAUSEWAY. – I've not, it's you, I don't, I never, what makes you think so—?

(He begins to wipe up the mess.)

LILY. – Maybe I'm mistaken?   **MR. CAUSEWAY** *(Protesting too much)* – No. But I would never—

LILY. – But I wonder?
...No forget it—   **MR. CAUSEWAY** – No, what?

*(**MR. CAUSEWAY** talks to **LILY** but she is mostly talking to herself.)*

LILY. – I liked it when I didn't have all these questions in my head. My mother used to say, 'you've got an answer for everything'. I don't know anything anymore—

MR. CAUSEWAY. – Did I?… How did I give myself away?—

LILY. – I put everything in a neat little box, I didn't like the mess it caused—

MR. CAUSEWAY. – Did I stare? I didn't. If anything/[I *avoided* looking]—

LILY. – But *people* won't be tidied will they?!

MR. CAUSEWAY. – I wasn't seeing you in the altogether or any such—

LILY. I expected Alan to be a good son, polite, you know, not let me down—

MR. CAUSEWAY. It was more from admiration—

LILY. – What does that even mean? 'Not let me down'?

MR. CAUSEWAY. – Not that seeing you in the altogether would put me off or/[anything]—

LILY. How can you let someone down you never promised anything to—

MR. CAUSEWAY. – You're a formidable woman, Lillian—

LILY. – He's his own person, he doesn't owe me nothing—

MR. CAUSEWAY. But you were taken so I never said/ [anything]—

LILY. – I never saw it like that but he's forced me to look at it now—

MR. CAUSEWAY. But sometimes, you know, when you're on the phone—

LILY. And I wonder what I've been doing all these years—

MR. CAUSEWAY. – It seems like they are being forced into submission—

LILY. – Why was I married to a man I bloody hated? And worse, why did I do what he said? I mean, I'm not a trained gorilla am I—?

MR. CAUSEWAY. – Like they've got no choice. *I've* got no choice—

LILY. – It's not black and white that's for sure—

MR. CAUSEWAY. – But I am relieved that it's finally out in the open—

(She looks at him.)

LILY. – I want to fix this. Do you think it's too late to start again? At my age—

(He is overcome.)

MR. CAUSEWAY. – I know we're not young but there's no reason why we can't enjoy ourselves you know—

LILY. – I think I should try, I'd like to try—

MR. CAUSEWAY. *(delighted)* Would you?

LILY. That's why I asked—

MR. CAUSEWAY. – Would Saturday night be too/[soon]?

LILY. *(to him, serious)* – If I reminded you of your mother?

MR. CAUSEWAY. – My mother! You're nothing like my mother, my mother couldn't boil an egg—!

LILY. *(in her own world again)* – Tch, you think I'm talking nonsense, I probably am—

MR. CAUSEWAY. – No! You're making perfect sense only please leave my mother out of it. It sort of clouds the issue and puts me off—

LILY. – Fine.

(She turns away.)

MR. CAUSEWAY. – I'll book a table for Saturday then, at that French place on the high street, L'Etoile?/[seven o'clock]—

(She goes to leave.)

LILY. – I'm going to give Alan a call, give me a line will you?

MR. CAUSEWAY. Yes … *my dear.*

(She gives him a quizzical look and exits. He punches his fist into his hand.)

Too soon.

(In the call room.)

TIFFANY. Tea, Mr. C?

*(**MR. CAUSEWAY** is wringing his hands in embarrassment.)*

MR. CAUSEWAY. Not now, thank you, Tiffany.

*(**LILY** readies herself for the call.)*

LILY. If not now, then when?

(Lily is lit, the rest of the stage is in darkness.)

(She swallows hard and dials the number. Part way through **LILY**'s *conversation* **TIFFANY** *becomes aware of (***LILY**'s *distress. She gets up and quietly makes her a cup of tea.)*

Hello? Alan?… It's Mum. I've rung more times now than I ever have… You there?… Right, I just wanted to say, you know, when you weren't at the funeral— No, please, I'm not having a go… I mean I just rang to say, no, what I rang to say is… I don't blame you… Oh dear, I mean I think I understand, the phone calls, they are awkward. *(She gives a little laugh.)* But I told myself that you and me, we were doing quite well. I mean I couldn't really abide *my* mother so, well, at least we were civil. *(Almost to herself)* Haven't aimed very high have I?… I just thought I'd tell you that. *(Long pause)* Are you still there? … Well anyway. You're right, I don't know about you and that. What you do, what your hobbies are, what you think, or even if you still like rice pudding. *(Lily is struck by the fact that knowing he liked rice pudding is the last time she really knew anything about him.)* … I'd like to… I don't want to put no pressure on. *(Tries to be light, but is choked)* So, that's all, son. If you think you could bear to, you know, try again or something, that's it… If you don't, well, I respect that… Stay well… I love you, you know, even if I didn't always show it. *(Holding back the tears)* You know where I am, if, you know, you want anything. Bye then.

(Lights on **LILY** *for a while)*

(As she sits in solitude and swallows her tears, **TIFFANY** *sets the tea down in front of* **LILY** *and gently places a hand on her shoulder.* **LILY** *reaches up and gratefully takes it.)*

(Lights fade.)

(Lights up on:)

Scene Five

(A new day. **LILY** *is once again salesperson of the month for November.)*

(There is a sparkly 'Happy Christmas' banner up at the back of the room and a load of large brown boxes with the words 'Vagimix, an assortment of pleasure toys for her', written on the side.)

*(***MR. CAUSEWAY***'s office has the door and hatch closed. We see his reactions to what happens in the call room.* **LILY** *and* **TIFFANY** *are peering into one of the boxes.)*

LILY. It's not right, I mean it's the same old shit but they shouldn't confuse this nonsense with kitchen goods, it's unhygienic.

*(***TIFFANY*** *emerges.)*

TIFFANY. You wouldn't get confused.

*(***LILY*** *pulls out a pink, whisk-like implement.)*

LILY. It's not black and it's not leather. I could hang this in my kitchen and no one would be any the wiser.

*(***LILY*** *makes a whisking action.)*

TIFFANY. Well it's not like food and sex don't mix, Ben likes to/[rub cream]—

*(***LILY*** *holds her hand up like Arnie in "Terminator".)*

LILY. Thank you, Tiffany, talk to the face.

TIFFANY. What?

LILY. You heard.

TIFFANY. No, it's the hand, you say talk to the hand when you're not listening.

LILY. I'm not.

TIFFANY. No – wha—

LILY. My point is, if I mix up my sexual aid with my Kitchenaid, you wouldn't know if my fondant fancies were untainted would you?

TIFFANY. I've never tasted your fondant fancies, but I've tasted Victoria's sponge.

*(**TIFFANY** grabs a dildo and chases **LILY** around the room poking it at her bottom. **LILY** runs away laughing.)*

Don't s'pose you've felt one of these in a while!

LILY. Put it away, you silly mare.

*(**LILY** stops outside **MR. CAUSEWAY**'s door, breathless.)*

Did he come out when I was in the wotsit?

*(**LILY** indicates the toilet. **TIFFANY** shakes her head and looks at her watch.)*

TIFFANY. It's nearly lunchtime and I'm still waiting for the order number, I dunno what they cost or *nothing*.

*(**LILY** knocks on the door.)*

LILY. You alright in there?

MR. CAUSEWAY. *(overly light)* I'm a bit tied up at the minute.

LILY. You're not testing the merchandise are you?

*(**TIFFANY** laughs. He squirms.)*

Can't tempt you with a slice of Madeira?

MR. CAUSEWAY. No thank you.

*(**LILY** and **TIFFANY** exchange looks.)*

LILY. Can I come in?

(He panics and starts piling his desk with spreadsheets.)

MR. CAUSEWAY. Er, er, um.

LILY. Oh for goodness sake, I'm coming in, pull your trousers up.

(He gasps silently then opens the door.)

MR. CAUSEWAY. I wasn't doing anything of the sort. As you can see, end of year figures, I'm a bit snowed under.

LILY. That's as maybe but I've never known you refuse cake. You under the weather?

MR. CAUSEWAY. I'm fine, please don't concern yourself.

(He closes the door after she leaves. **LILY** *is nonplussed by his odd behaviour. She is about to commence knitting the pink bootees that are on her needles but gets back up and knocks on his door again. He opens it a tad.)*

LILY. I think you should come over to me for Christmas.

MR. CAUSEWAY. Sorry?

LILY. You'll be on your own.

MR. CAUSEWAY. Err, yes but there's nothing unusual about that.

LILY. Well then.

MR. CAUSEWAY. It would be too much trouble.

LILY. How could it be trouble, I'll be cooking it anyway. *(Pause)* Come to think of it, if you don't come I'll have no reason to cook it.

(The fact that they she will be alone sinks in. **LILY** *is suddenly coy.)*

Now there's a thought.

MR. CAUSEWAY. *(he swallows)* I waited until half past nine.

LILY. What?

MR. CAUSEWAY. On Saturday.

*(***LILY** *looks confused.* **TIFFANY** *twigs.)*

TIFFANY. Oh – my – god. You stood him up!

LILY. What?

MR. CAUSEWAY. It's nothing.

LILY. What do you mean?

MR. CAUSEWAY. – Forget it.

TIFFANY. You are well bad.

LILY. – Did you ask me to go/[out]—

TIFFANY. Duh, Sherlock.

LILY. Be quiet, Tiffany.   **MR. CAUSEWAY.** It's really not important.

LILY. When?

MR. CAUSEWAY. What?

LILY. When did you ask?

MR. CAUSEWAY. – The other day, but it's really of no consequence.

LILY. You know I'd never do such a thing.

(The pain on **MR. CAUSEWAY***'s face begins to dissipate. He opens the door more fully.)*

I mean if I didn't want to meet someone I'd tell them straight wouldn't I?

TIFFANY. She would an' all.

MR. CAUSEWAY. Yes! I believe you would.

LILY. I'm ever so sorry for the misunderstanding—

MR. CAUSEWAY. – It was a silly idea anyway—

LILY. – No, not totally.

*(***LILY** *looks at the floor.)*

MR. CAUSEWAY. No?

*(***TIFFANY** *looks on, amused.)*

(Long awkward pause.)

LILY. No one's ever waited for me before.

MR. CAUSEWAY. *(mumbles)* I can't think why.

(Awkward pause.)

LILY. It's not easy is it? Change.

MR. CAUSEWAY. No, no it isn't.

LILY. So, Christmas. I can make it up to you?

MR. CAUSEWAY. If you're sure?

LILY. – Oh for goodness' sake, we're never going to get/ [anywhere like this]—

MR. CAUSEWAY. – I accept.

*(***LILY** *walks away smiling.* **TIFFANY** *nudges* **LILY***.)*

TIFFANY. Re-sult.

(**LILY** *shoos her away, but likes it.* **MR. CAUSEWAY** *does a private, restrained jig in his office.*)

(**MR. CAUSEWAY** *pokes his head out of the door.*)

MR. CAUSEWAY. Actually I could eat a slice of Victoria sponge if it's still going? No sense in working non-stop.

(*He goes back to his desk.*)

LILY. It's Madeira.

TIFFANY. He'll never notice, state he's in.

(*They laugh.* **MR. CAUSEWAY** *enters the call room.*)

MR. CAUSEWAY. Lillian. It's Alan.

LILY. God.

(**LILY** *enters his office. She is about to answer but falters. She tidies her hair and smooths her dress.* **MR. CAUSEWAY** *gives her some privacy.*)

Hello… Yes…no…no… I wasn't expecting… Thursday? Yes, yes I would, of course I do. Wait!… Alan… I'm *really* pleased you asked.

(*The call ends.* **LILY** *enters the call room.* **MR. CAUSEWAY** *and* **TIFFANY** *are expectant.*)

MR. CAUSEWAY. Well?

LILY. We're going to meet for tea, just for a chat.

MR. CAUSEWAY. That's very good news.   **TIFFANY.** That's brill.

LILY. It's just a chat, I mustn't get my hopes up. Still, it's a good sign isn't it?

MR. CAUSEWAY. It's a very good sign.

LILY. We should celebrate. I've got some Avocat in me bag. I was saving it for Christmas.

TIFFANY. I'm not drinking that, whatever it is.

MR. CAUSEWAY. Let's go and get something else then, Tiffany. I must admit, it's not my favourite tipple. I'll get twenty pounds from the float.

(**TIFFANY** *and* **LILY** *exchange excited squeals.*)

(**JANICE** *enters. She takes in the jolly scene.*)

JANICE. What's going on?

LILY. We're celebrating.

JANICE. What we celebrating?

TIFFANY. Christmas! Alan rang Lily, and *(privately to* **JANICE***)* come to the offy, you are *not* going to believe what I'm gonna tell ya. *(So everyone can hear)* Mr. C is giving us twenty-five quid from the float.

JANICE. This day just keeps getting better. Guess what? Me and Jim went for *brunch,* just the two of us, no kids…

LILY. Well then. Get crisps and nuts if this is going to be a party.

(**MR. CAUSEWAY** *and* **TIFFANY** *put their coats on.*)

MR. CAUSEWAY. *(shy)* Is there anything special you'd like, Lillian?

(**LILY** *is equally bashful and unused to it.*)

LILY. No thank you … Cecil … I'll be washing these filthy glasses.

(**TIFFANY** *nudges* **JANICE** *and mouths the word 'Cecil'.*)

JANICE. What the—?

TIFFANY. I told you.

(*The sound of excited banter as they leave the building.*)

(**LILY** *is alone. She begins to wash cups and lay a table for the imminent party. She hears someone outside.*)

LILY. What have you forgotten?

(**SYLVIE** *appears with a push chair.*)

Sylvie.

SYLVIE. *(dull, confrontational)* Yes I'm back.

LILY. Is that—?

SYLVIE. Yes.

LILY. You going to introduce us, then?

(**SYLVIE** *takes a cigarette from the baby-changing bag hooked on the pram. She is full of bravado and swagger.*)

SYLVIE. *(confronting)* Do you think Mr. Causeway will smell the smoke if I do it in there?

(Indicates the toilet)

LILY. You don't smoke.

(**SYLVIE** *shrugs and walks to the toilet and lights up. She talks to* **LILY** *from the toilet doorway.*)

SYLVIE. I do now.

(**LILY** *walks toward the pram.* **SYLVIE** *is alarmed.*)

Don't wake her.

(**LILY** *backs off a little.*)

LILY. Janice said you were collecting her.

(**SYLVIE** *wafts the smoke away.* **LILY** *peers into the pram from a distance.*)

Can't see much of her.

(*As* **LILY** *approaches the pram,* **SYLVIE** *stiffens.*)

SYLVIE. Don't!… She just went to sleep.

(**LILY** *walks away sensing* **SYLVIE***'s panic.*)

LILY. So, Guatemala was it?

SYLVIE. Yes.

LILY. You must be pleased.

SYLVIE. *(sarcastic, nonchalant)* It's like getting a new dress. Well not a new one, a second-hand one. You know, you have to try it on and see, will it fit. For sure no one else will have the same one, it's a one-off… So it's not couture but it did fit me and…they wrapped her up and—

(*She points at the pram. The baby whimpers.* **SYLVIE** *tries to maintain indifference but we can tell she is on red alert.*)

She can't wake up yet.

LILY. You been back long?

SYLVIE. Fifteen days. Today is sixteen. *(Panic)* What does she want?

> *(She rests the cigarette on the sink in readiness to go to the pram.)*

LILY. Maybe she's just having a little dream.

SYLVIE. They dream?

LILY. I meant, it's only a whimper.

> *(**LILY** watches **SYLVIE**, concerned.)*

> This your first time out with her?

> *(**SYLVIE** nods and picks up the cigarette.)*

SYLVIE. I didn't manage to wash yesterday.

LILY. Her?

SYLVIE. Myself.

LILY. I remember that.

SYLVIE. *(a ray of hope)* Really?

LILY. They're always wanting something—

SYLVIE. Davide went back to work, he left me alone with her.

LILY. Mmm, it's not easy is it?

> *(**SYLVIE** shakes her head.)*

> I bet she can give it some welly if she wants.

SYLVIE. What does that mean?

LILY. I only meant, I bet she can make a noise.

SYLVIE. It's like a big banging in my head. I can't bear it. *(Pause)* I don't tell anyone but I can tell you. *I don't want this baby.*

> *(**LILY** tries not to look alarmed.)*

> *(**SYLVIE** can't settle (like the baby). She puts the cigarette down again and walks to the crib. The baby quietens. She walks away again.)*

LILY. That's how you feel now—

SYLVIE. *(wishing it were true)* I don't *feel* anything.

LILY. You're angry though.

SYLVIE. Yes angry, I do feel like that.

LILY. And a bit afraid?

(The women look at each other for some moments.)

(The baby whimpers intermittently. **SYLVIE** *visibly tenses every time it makes a sound.)*

SYLVIE. I leave her?

LILY. It depends what she wants—

SYLVIE. *(panic)* I don't know what she wants.

(She throws the cigarette on the floor and walks to the pram. She talks into the pram from an upright position looking down into it.)

(Said almost like a question to the child) I just fed you.

(The baby makes a louder noise. She pleads to **LILY***.)*

You want to hold her?

*(***LILY*** is about to then stops herself.)*

LILY. I can't, love, I need to spend a penny. I might wet myself if I pick her up.

SYLVIE. *(demanding)* So go then.

LILY. I will in a second. *(Deflecting)* So how it's been—?

SYLVIE. Terrible.

LILY. These things take/[time]—

SYLVIE. NO! She doesn't need *me.*

LILY. If she doesn't need you then who?

(Long pause. **SYLVIE** *is less aggressive which gives way to the sadness.)*

SYLVIE. I thought it would be different. I thought that I would be the most important person in the world to her but I can't help her, not at all.

LILY. If you send her back someone else will have to get to know her, love her.

SYLVIE. Let them.

*(The baby cries. **SYLVIE** looks at **LILY**, desperate for help.)*

Do something.

LILY. What happens when I'm not around, when no one is around?

SYLVIE. *(almost in tears, loud)* Exactly! Why isn't anyone listening to me? You think it will go away this feeling. It's not getting better, it's getting worse. I don't want to be left alone with her.

LILY. Just because you give birth, doesn't mean you know what to do, and being a mum is scary.

SYLVIE. You're just saying it to make me feel better but it won't work.

LILY. Seriously. You want to accuse *me* of that?

SYLVIE. I'm not a mother.

LILY. You're *her* mother.

SYLVIE. I'm not. I don't know what to do, I don't know what she wants, what she needs.*(Hopeless)* If I was her mother I would know what to do. I'm no good.

*(**SYLVIE** rattles the pram out of desperation.)*

LILY. It's not automatic, you know. No matter how motherly a woman is, she doesn't *know*. She just goes through a checklist and hopes for the best. They can't talk, *none of them*!

SYLVIE. This is *not* a joke.

LILY. I know.

SYLVIE. But me, what was I thinking?

LILY. I felt like you do.

*(**SYLVIE** is surprised.)*

I was in shock when Alan arrived. Here was this stranger in my arms. I thought, 'and I'm meant to look after *you* for the next eighteen years? I don't even know you'.

SYLVIE. Please, please don't say things to try and make me feel normal.

LILY. I'm not saying it's nothing, it's mammoth. If she's lucky you'll see to all of her needs, feed her when she needs feeding, change her when she needs changing. But the only thing that really matters is if you can love her.

SYLVIE. *(hopeful)* But…will she…need me?

LILY. Oh she needs you. Believe me, she'll need you so much that every word you say or don't say will mean something. Everything you do and don't do, she'll make it mean something about her. There will be so much significance attached to you, you can't imagine. People can criticise the way you look after her and say you should do this or you should have done that but if you love him, he should know that … and if he doesn't then you will have done your best and you will have to hope that it was enough.

(Long pause)

SYLVIE. You mean her?

*(**LILY** nods.)*

LILY. Anyway, we're just guardians I reckon. 'Til they're ready to bugger off.

SYLVIE. Guardians?

*(The two women look into the pram. **SYLVIE** looks helpless but like she wants what **LILY** is saying to be true. **LILY** guides **SYLVIE** nearer to the pram.)*

LILY. I think she's looking at you.

SYLVIE. *(yearning)* Really?

LILY. She is.

*(**LILY** gently moves the blanket aside and invites **SYLVIE** to pick the baby up. **SYLVIE** hesitates then gingerly takes the baby out of the pram. She looks to **LILY** for reassurance. **LILY** gives it. **SYLVIE** holds the baby. It quietens. She turns the baby and looks into her face.)*

SYLVIE. *(gentle)* If I'm the guardian I guess she can call me maman…for now.

LILY. And she'll call you a lot more besides.

(The irony is lost on **SYLVIE** *because she is starting to fall in love.* **LILY** *watches over her shoulder.)*

*(***SYLVIE** *is moved by the baby for the first time, and does not take her eyes off her.)*

SYLVIE. I suppose I will have to do.

LILY. You'll do fine.

(We can hear the sound of the others returning.)

(Lights fade.)

The End

Lightning Source UK Ltd.
Milton Keynes UK
UKHW021258071222
413539UK00034B/351